Weight Watchers™

STORE CUPBOARD COOKING

LESLEY WATERS

SIMON & SCHUSTER
A VIACOM COMPANY

First published in Great Britain by Simon & Schuster, 1997
A Viacom Company

Simon & Schuster Ltd
West Garden Place
Kendal Street
London W2 2AQ

Design: Moore Lowenhoff
Cover design: Jane Humphrey
Typesetting: Stylize
Photography: Steve Lee
Styling: Marion McLornan
Food preparation: Joanna Craig

Weight Watchers Publications Manager: Juliet Hudson
Weight Watchers Publications Assistant: Celia Whiston

A CIP catalogue record is available from the British Library

ISBN 0 68482 115 X

Printed and bound in Italy by Rotolito Lombarda S.p.A.

Pictured on the front cover: *Scotch Broth (page 24)*

Pictured on the back cover: *Lentil Sag with Raisin and Mint Raita (page 59)*

Recipe notes:
Egg size is medium, unless otherwise stated.
Vegetables are medium-sized, unless otherwise stated.
It is important to use proper measuring spoons, not cutlery, for spoon measures.
1 tablespoon = 15 ml; 1 teaspoon = 5 ml.
Dried herbs can be substituted for fresh ones, but the flavour may not always
be as good. Halve the fresh-herb quantity stated in the recipe.

Contents

Introduction	4
Light Meals, Starters and Snacks	8
One-Pot Meals	20
Main Meal Salads	31
Feasts from the Sea	39
Main Courses	52
Fabulous Puddings	64
Delicious Bakes	76
Index	80

Introduction

Weight Watchers *Store Cupboard Cooking* is designed to follow the *1,2,3 Success*™ Programme, which lets you enjoy the foods you love and helps you lose weight at the same time.

This book is for anyone who enjoys good food but doesn't want to spend hours in the kitchen or a fortune on ingredients. It's full of delicious home cooking that is fast and a pleasure to serve to family and friends. You'll have fun putting these recipes together with store cupboard ingredients; you'll also probably find that a well stocked store cupboard will allow you to be more creative and spontaneous in the kitchen.

The Store Cupboard

Although a store cupboard sounds old-fashioned, it is actually perfect for the modern kitchen and today's busy cooks who want to create fabulous food fast. An organised store cupboard, full of interesting and versatile ingredients, is the secret to delicious food in minutes. Here are a few tips on how to get the most out of your store cupboard.

A Store Cupboard for All Seasons

Using space well

1. Free some cupboard space in your store cupboard by taking out the pots and pans and using poles and hooks to suspend your saucepans from the wall or ceiling.

2. Throw away any pans, baking trays or roasting tins which you haven't used for a while and have seen better days.

3. Clear out any food which is past its sell-by date and sort out your freezer, getting rid of any suspicious-looking ingredients.

4. Pack away any kitchen equipment that you no longer use and that quirky Christmas present which has been shoved to the back of the cupboard…

Quick stock checks

1. Organise your cupboard space so that your jars, cans, flavourings and spices all have their own space. This makes it easier to do quick stock checks before a shopping trip and prevents you from wasting time rummaging through every cupboard to look for that important ingredient.

2. For less perishable fruit and vegetables, such as potatoes, carrots and onions, save valuable fridge space by storing them in a plastic box in a dark, cool spot under the stairs, cellar, or even in the shed or garage.

3. Divide your fridge into various sections, such as dairy, cooked and uncooked ingredients and salad ingredients. Once again, this will make life easier when you do the last minute stock check.

4. Organise your freezer in the same order as your fridge: date and label clearly all frozen vegetables, raw fish, raw meat and cooked items. Most importantly, make sure they are wrapped well.

Build up your stores gradually, adding a few things every week. Eventually, you will have a larder which saves you time and money and brings a sense of adventure into your kitchen!

Kitchen cupboard suggestions:

Here are some suggestions for your store cupboard, which will help you to make the recipes in this book. Of course, you don't need to have all of them: it's up to you to decide what you want to have on hand.

Rice: Easy-cook brown rice, short-grain or long-grain rice, basmati, white or brown long-grain canned rice (yes, it really does exist!).

Grains: Bulgar wheat for salads and pilaffs, pearl barley for thickening and adding to stews or soups. Porridge oats make a nutritious breakfast but they're also delicious in crumble toppings on top of sweet or savoury dishes, not to mention in cakes and stuffings.

Flour: Wholemeal and plain flour, self-raising flour and cornflour are all a must but, remember, flour doesn't keep well so buy it in small quantities and check the 'use-by' date.
Dried Pasta and Noodles: Spaghetti, tagliatelle, quills, tubes, macaroni, wholemeal pasta for soups, stuffing and baking. If the pasta is egg-free, this will reduce the fat content so be sure to check this on the packaging. Pasta with eggs isn't really ideal to store, since it doesn't keep as long. Chinese egg and rice noodles are versatile standbys, so don't overlook them. Store dried pasta and noodles in their own packages; glass jars are not good for storing.
Pulses: Haricot beans, flageolet beans, chick-peas, green lentils, red kidney beans. The wide selection available today of canned, cooked pulses is so convenient; they only need to be rinsed and drained to be made into tasty and nourishing dishes in minutes.
Bread and Crispbreads: Pizza dough bases, corn taco shells, wheat tortillas, pitta breads, rice cakes and rye breads. All these can become the basis of quick and delicious lunches or suppers.
Nuts and Seeds: Sesame seeds, poppy seeds, sunflower seeds, hazelnuts, cashew nuts and chestnuts are not as high in Points as some other ingredients in this category. Although generally considered undesirable in a low-fat diet, they can be eaten in moderation and will add flavour and texture. They are also a good source of energy. Seeds and nuts should be stored in an airtight container and bought in small quantities since they do not keep as well as some other store cupboard items.
Fruit: Prunes, apricots, dates, sultanas and currants all have unlimited uses.
Oils: Olive oil, sunflower oil, sesame oil and low-fat spray oil (for greasing). Keep oils out of direct sunlight, store in a cool, dark place and keep the lid tightly screwed on to the bottle. Beware of the 'use-by' date: oil well past this date will lose its flavour and could turn rancid.
Spices (see lists below): Always buy in small quantities, especially if they are ground. Always store in an airtight glass jar, well away from heat and light, and don't keep for longer than six months.
Whole Spices: Whole black peppercorns, cinnamon sticks, nutmeg, coriander seeds and cardamom pods.

Ground Spices: Coriander, turmeric, garam masala, paprika, ginger, cumin and chilli.
Dried Herbs: Oregano, thyme, bay leaves, dill weed and sage: these herbs keep well when they are dried. Fresh herbs, however, are always preferable and are widely available in supermarkets now. If you have any leftover herbs from your garden this summer, freeze them so that you have a store to draw on all year round.
Canned Vegetables: Beansprouts, peas, mushrooms, water chestnuts, baby corn, artichoke hearts, red pimientos and new potatoes (with the skins on are best) are very useful indeed. There are many varieties of the essential canned tomatoes: chopped tomatoes with herbs or chillies, cherry tomatoes, plum tomatoes and, of course, cream tomatoes, which are excellent for sauces. For a treat, have some *anti pasti* peppers, artichokes in brine, olives, sun-dried tomatoes or dried (porcini) mushrooms on hand.
Canned Fish: Red or pink salmon, tuna fish in brine, sardines, clams or crab meat.
Canned Fruit: For when you fancy a pudding, have a supply on hand of your favourite fruits preserved in their natural juice. A good supply of jam is always useful too.
Sugars: Caster sugar, muscovado sugar, icing sugar, runny honey and marmalade.
Sauces and Condiments: Worcestershire sauce, chilli sauce, soy sauce, sun-dried tomato paste, curry paste, red and white wine vinegar, coarse-grain mustard, Dijon mustard, yeast extract, mint sauce, horseradish sauce, black bean sauce, pesto sauce, vegetable, beef and chicken stock cubes, garlic purée, vanilla essence and cocoa powder.
Fresh Vegetables and Fruit: Potatoes, onions, carrots, lemons, oranges, bananas, apples, pears and a string of garlic. All these staples keep well as long as they are stored in a cool, dark place.
For the Fridge: lean bacon, low-fat mature Cheddar cheese, low-fat cream cheese, low-fat fromage frais, low-fat natural yogurt, polyunsaturated margarine, salad ingredients, semi-skimmed and skimmed milk, and tomato salsa.
For the Freezer: lamb mince, chicken breasts, pork chops, frozen fish fillets, a selection of frozen vegetables, summer berry mix and filo pastry.

Light Meals, Starters and Snacks

Here are some quick and tasty recipes which you can enjoy as a snack, starter or meal, depending on what you fancy. They're almost as easy as opening a can of vegetables or fruit but the taste is much, much more exciting! Do you long for some tacos, an omelette, or some scrumptious potato skins? Well, with these recipes, satisfying that craving is almost as easy as 1,2,3!

Butter Bean Chilli Tacos

Serves 6

Preparation and cooking time: 25 minutes
Calories per serving: 200

Freezing: not recommended

Serve these tasty butter beans on toast or as a filling for baked potatoes or taco shells.

½ tablespoon olive oil
1 large onion, chopped
1 garlic clove, crushed
2 × 420 g (14 oz) can of butter beans, or any other canned, cooked pulse, drained and rinsed
juice of 1 lemon
420 g (14 oz) can of chopped tomatoes
480 g (1 lb) carton of creamed tomatoes
2 teaspoons brown sugar
1 tablespoon coarse-grain mustard
Tabasco sauce, to taste
salt and freshly ground black pepper
To serve:
6 taco shells
crisp salad leaves
150 ml (5 fl oz) low-fat natural yogurt

1. In a large saucepan, heat the oil. Add the onion and fry until softened. Add the garlic and butter beans and fry for a further 2 minutes.
2. Add the lemon juice, canned tomatoes, creamed tomatoes and sugar. Season well.
3. Bring the contents of the pan to the boil and simmer gently for 15 minutes.
4. Stir in the mustard and add Tabasco sauce to taste.
5. To serve, warm the taco shells as directed on the packet.
6. Fill the taco shells with crisp salad leaves, spoon over the hot beans and drizzle over a little yogurt. Serve at once.

Points per serving: 2½
Total Points per recipe: 15

Pear, Poppy Seed and Cheese Bap

Serves 4

Preparation and cooking time: 10 minutes
Calories per serving: 435

Freezing: not recommended

The combination of pears and blue cheese topped with poppy seeds is mouth-watering; however, if blue cheese is not to your taste you can use low-fat Cheddar or Edam instead. The Points will be as follows: with low-fat Cheddar and fromage frais, 7½ Points per serving and with low-fat Cheddar and yogurt, 6½ Points per serving. Edam with fromage frais is 8½ Points per serving and with yogurt is 7½ Points.

2 large Granary baps
4 medium slices of ham, cut into strips
4 tablespoons low-fat fromage frais or low-fat natural yogurt
2 teaspoons coarse-grain mustard
150 g (5 oz) Danish blue cheese, crumbled
1 large ripe pear, cored and sliced thinly or 2 canned pear halves in natural juice, sliced
freshly ground black pepper
1 tablespoon poppy seeds (optional)
To serve:
mustard and watercress salad or a salad of your choice

1. Preheat the grill.
2. Split and toast the baps.
3. In a bowl, combine the ham, fromage frais, mustard and three-quarters of the cheese. Spread this mixture over the toasted baps and top with the pear slices.
4. Sprinkle the baps with the remaining cheese, grind over the black pepper and place under a moderately hot grill for 3–4 minutes, until bubbling and golden.
5. Remove from the grill and sprinkle with poppy seeds. Serve at once with the salad of your choice.

Points per serving: with yogurt 8½; with fromage frais 9½
Total Points per recipe: with yogurt 34; with fromage frais 38

Lattice Potatoes

Serves 4

Preparation time: 10 minutes
Cooking time: 50 minutes
Calories per serving: 225

Freezing: not recommended

A favourite with a twist – you'll love the tasty sauces for dipping! Be sure to check the Points for different brands of tomato salsa or houmous.

480 g (1 lb) medium potatoes, scrubbed
2 tablespoons olive oil
3 tablespoons dark soy sauce
1 teaspoon dried thyme
salt and freshly ground black pepper
To serve:
1 apple, diced finely
1/2 teaspoon dried thyme
226 g jar of tomato salsa

1. Preheat the oven to Gas Mark 6/200°C/400°F.
2. Cut the potatoes in half lengthways and, using a small, sharp knife, cut into the flesh in a lattice fashion, without cutting through the potato skin.
3. In a large bowl, toss the potatoes in the olive oil, soy sauce and dried thyme. Season well. Turn into a large, shallow roasting tray or oven dish, and cover with foil. Bake in the oven for 30 minutes.
4. Remove the foil and cook for a further 15–20 minutes or until the potatoes are golden and crisp.
5. Meanwhile, add the diced apple and thyme to the tomato salsa and set aside.
6. To serve, pile the hot potatoes on to a platter and serve with a bowl of salsa for dipping.

Points per serving: 4
Total Points per recipe: 16

Variation:
Instead of the salsa, you could serve the potatoes with 165 g (5 1/2 oz) of reduced-fat houmous. This would increase the Points to 4 1/2 per serving.

Potato, Ham and Apple Frittata

Serves 4

Preparation and cooking time: 25 minutes
Calories per serving: with ham 295; with bacon 310

Freezing: not recommended

Perfect for a weekend brunch or a light midweek meal, served with a salad.

1 1/2 tablespoons olive oil
1 large onion, sliced
1 large potato, washed and grated
2 medium apples, peeled, cored and sliced thinly
5 eggs
1 teaspoon dried thyme
3 slices of lean ham or smoked bacon, chopped
2 tablespoons grated Parmesan or any strong cheese of your choice
2 tablespoons chopped fresh parsley (optional)
salt and freshly ground black pepper

1. Preheat the grill.
2. In a large, non-stick frying-pan, heat 1 tablespoon of the olive oil and fry the onion until softened. Using kitchen paper, dry the excess water from the potato. Add the potato to the onion and fry for 3–4 minutes. Transfer to a plate and leave to cool slightly.
3. In the frying-pan, heat the remaining 1/2 tablespoon of olive oil. Add the apples and cook for 2–3 minutes.
4. In a mixing bowl, beat the eggs with the thyme and season well. Add the cooled potato mixture. Transfer this mixture to the pan with the apples and chopped ham or bacon. Fry gently for 8–10 minutes over a low heat.
5. Sprinkle the cheese and parsley over the frittata and place under the grill until the top is golden brown and the frittata is set.
6. Serve the frittata cut into wedges, hot, warm or cold.

Points per serving: with bacon 7; with ham 6
Total Points per recipe: with bacon 28; with ham 24

Chick-Pea Burgers

Serves 4

Preparation and cooking time: 15 minutes + 30 minutes chilling
Calories per serving: with sweet and sour sauce 420; with tzatziki 400; with barbecue 410

Freezing: not recommended

These moist burgers are flavoured with hazelnuts for a very interesting taste and are delicious served hot or cold. You can serve these with a wide variety of sauces but be sure to check the Points for different brands because they do differ.

420 g (14 oz) can of chick-peas, drained and rinsed
120 g (4 oz) hazelnuts, chopped
1 onion, chopped finely
2 carrots, grated
2 tablespoons tomato purée
2 tablespoons Worcestershire sauce
1 egg
2 tablespoons dried wholemeal breadcrumbs, for coating
freshly ground black pepper
To serve:
crisp lettuce leaves
tomatoes, sliced
low-fat salad dressing
200 g jar of sweet and sour sauce or barbecue sauce or 170 g (5½ oz) tzatziki

1. In a large bowl, mash the drained chick-peas with a potato masher.
2. Stir in the hazelnuts, onion, carrots, tomato purée, Worcestershire sauce and egg. Mix well. Season to taste.
3. Shape the mixture into 4 flat burgers and lightly sprinkle with the breadcrumbs. Place in the fridge to chill for 30 minutes.
4. Preheat the grill. Grill the burgers for 3–4 minutes on each side, turning carefully.
5. Serve the chick-pea burgers with a salad of lightly dressed lettuce and tomato slices and your choice of sauces.

Points per serving: with sweet and sour sauce 7; with tzatziki 7; with barbecue sauce 6½
Total Points per recipe: with sweet and sour sauce 28; with tzatziki 28; with barbecue sauce 26

Sardine Muffin Toasts

Serves 4

Preparation and cooking time: 10 minutes
Calories per serving: 145

Freezing: not recommended

If you think you don't like sardines, try these and think again!

2 muffins
2 × 120 g can of sardines in tomato sauce (skinless and boneless, if available)
1 tablespoon mild curry paste
freshly ground black pepper
To serve:
salad leaves
2 tablespoons mango or lime chutney

1. Preheat the grill.
2. Toast the muffins on both sides.
3. In a bowl, mash the sardines and combine with the curry paste. Split the muffins in half and spread each half with the sardine mixture. Grind over some black pepper.
4. Place the muffins under a moderate grill for 4–5 minutes or until bubbling and hot. Serve at once, surrounded by salad leaves, with the chutney on the side.

Points per serving: 4
Total Points per recipe: 16

Tortilla with Mexican Sauce

Serves 4

Preparation and cooking time: 10 minutes
Calories per serving: with avocado 415; without avocado 315

Freezing: not recommended

These tortillas are delicious and fun to eat. But make sure you have large napkins on hand!

8 flour tortillas
400 g can of tuna in brine, drained
1 small onion, chopped
a handful of crisp salad leaves, shredded
226 g jar of chilli tomato salsa
4 tablespoons low-fat natural yogurt
1 medium avocado, diced (optional)
salt and freshly ground black pepper
lemon wedges, to serve

1. Heat the tortillas according to the packet instructions.
2. Spoon the remaining ingredients into small serving bowls and place on a tray.
3. Give each person 2 warm tortillas and let them help themselves to the toppings which should be sprinkled on to each tortilla and then topped with a squeeze of lemon juice. Roll up to eat.

Points per serving: 6½; without avocado 5½
Total Points per recipe: 26; without avocado 22

Fast Salmon Pâté

Serves 6

Preparation time: 10 minutes
Calories per serving: 160

Freezing: not recommended

Serve with vegetable crudités, a selection of sesame crispbreads (add 1 Point for each crispbread), or a medium slice of Granary toast (add 1½ Points).

418 g can of red salmon, drained, with skin and bones discarded
180 g (6 oz) low-fat soft cheese flavoured with garlic and herbs
grated zest and juice of 1 lemon
2 teaspoons tomato purée
2 teaspoons olive oil
chopped fresh flat parsley (optional)
freshly ground black pepper

1. In a food processor or liquidiser, place the salmon, low-fat soft cheese, lemon zest, lemon juice and tomato purée. Blend until just smooth and season to taste.
2. Spoon the pâté into a serving dish and drizzle over the olive oil. Scatter with the parsley and grind over plenty of black pepper.
3. Place the dish of salmon pâté on a large platter or basket and surround with vegetable crudités, crispbreads or toast.

Points per serving: 3
Total Points per recipe: 18

White Bean Pâté with Horseradish

Serves 6

Preparation time: 15 minutes
Calories per serving: 95

Freezing: not recommended

Delicious and creamy. Serve with rye crackers or brown toast. Four rye crackers or two thin slices of brown toast will each add 2 Points per serving.

420 g can of butter beans, drained
3 teaspoons creamed horseradish
2 tablespoons olive oil
juice and zest of 1 lime or lemon
180 g (6 oz) frozen broad beans, cooked and peeled
2 tablespoons fresh flat-leaf parsley, leaves left whole (optional)
salt and freshly ground black pepper

1. Put three-quarters of the butter beans in a food processor with the horseradish, olive oil (reserving one teaspoon for the relish) and zest of lime or lemon. Season well. Whizz until smooth and creamy, adding a little warm water if necessary.
2. To make the relish, in a small bowl toss the remaining butter beans and broad beans with the lime or lemon juice, 1 teaspoon of olive oil and the parsley leaves, if using. Season to taste.
3. Pile the creamy pâté into a shallow serving dish or plate and scatter over the bean relish. Grind plenty of black pepper on top and chill until required.

Points per serving: 2
Total Points per recipe: 12

Eggs with Ratatouille

Serves 4

Preparation and cooking time: 20 minutes
Calories per serving: 175

Freezing: not recommended

Serve these with wholemeal toast (1½ Points per medium slice) or garlic bread (3½ Points per 5 cm/2-inch slice). The recipe for Garlic Toasts is on page 19.

1 tablespoon olive oil
1 large onion, sliced
240 g (8 oz) frozen sliced mixed peppers
1 tablespoon red pesto sauce
400 g can of cherry or chopped tomatoes
4 eggs
8 black olives, pitted and chopped roughly
1 tablespoon chopped fresh basil leaves (optional)
salt and freshly ground black pepper

1. In a large frying-pan, heat the olive oil. Fry the onion and peppers until coloured and softened. Stir in the red pesto sauce and cherry tomatoes. Season well and simmer for 3–4 minutes.
2. Using 2 wooden spoons, make 4 wells in the pan and crack an egg into each. Scatter over the olives, and basil if using, and season the eggs with freshly ground black pepper.
3. Reduce the heat and cover the pan. Cook for a further 3–5 minutes (depending on how you like your eggs cooked).

Points per serving: 2½
Total Points per recipe: 10

Omelette with Spinach, Tomatoes and Cheese

Serves 4

Preparation and cooking time: 20 minutes
Calories per serving: 270

Freezing: not recommended

This fluffy omelette is topped with the tasty combination of spinach and tomatoes. Delicious served with crusty bread.

1 tablespoon sunflower oil
1 large onion, sliced finely
180 g (6 oz) frozen chopped spinach
1 teaspoon freshly grated nutmeg
6 eggs
90 g (3 oz) low-fat mature Cheddar cheese, grated
1 tablespoon dried wholemeal breadcrumbs
360 g (12 oz) large tomatoes, sliced
4 tablespoons low-fat French dressing
salt and freshly ground black pepper

1. Preheat the grill.
2. In a large frying-pan, heat the oil and fry the onion until softened and coloured. Add the spinach and cook on a moderate heat to evaporate any excess water. Season with the nutmeg and black pepper.
3. In a bowl, beat the eggs with 2 tablespoons of water and season well. Add this to the pan and cook over a medium heat, until the omelette is set and lightly browned underneath.
4. Sprinkle the omelette with the cheese and breadcrumbs. Place under the grill until just firm on top. Remove from the grill, top with the tomato slices and spoon over the French dressing. Return to the grill until the tomatoes sizzle. Cut the omelette into wedges, take the pan to the table and serve at once.

Points per serving: 4½
Total Points per recipe: 18

Garlic Toasts

Makes 4

Preparation and cooking time: 5 minutes
Calories per serving: 80

Freezing: not recommended

These garlic toasts are a delicious low-fat alternative to garlic bread. Moist and tasty too, they are the ideal addition to any light meal or starter.

4 medium slices of Granary bread
2 fat garlic cloves, cut in half
freshly ground black pepper

1. Preheat the grill.
2. Toast the bread slices on both sides. While they're still hot, rub each piece of toast with a cut garlic clove and season with black pepper.
3. Serve at once.

Points per serving: 1½
Total Points per recipe: 6

One-Pot Meals

These recipes are all made in one pot which means that they're not only easy to make, but easy to clean up too. There's so little fuss and so much flavour here! The soups are warming, wholesome and tasty; the stews are so original and satisfying. These meals will give you the energy and bounce you want without all the extra fat and Calories, so bon appetit!

Seafood Soup

Serves 4

Preparation time: 10 minutes
Cooking time: 25 minutes
Calories per serving: 330

Freezing: not recommended

Steamed rice is a change from bread and makes a great accompaniment to this soup. Spoon a little on top just before serving. This will add 1½ Points per small portion.

½ tablespoon olive oil
1 onion, chopped
1 garlic clove, crushed
6 cardamom pods, crushed
5 cm (2-inch) strip of orange peel
1 bay leaf
270 g jar of mixed sliced peppers, drained and rinsed
1½ tablespoons sun-dried tomato paste or tomato purée
2 × 400 g can of chopped tomatoes
480 g (1 lb) frozen white flesh fish (e.g. haddock or cod), thawed and cut into large cubes
150 ml (¼ pint) white wine or water
180 g (6 oz) frozen peeled prawns, thawed
290 g can of clams, drained (optional)
salt and freshly ground black pepper
chopped fresh parsley, to garnish (optional)

1. In a large saucepan or wok, heat the olive oil and fry the onion until lightly browned.
2. Add the garlic, cardamom, orange peel, bay leaf and sliced peppers. Cook for a further 2 minutes.
3. Stir in the sun-dried tomato paste or purée, tomatoes and 150 ml (¼ pint) of water. Season well. Bring to the boil and simmer for 15–20 minutes.
4. Add the white fish and wine or water to the soup and simmer gently for 3–4 minutes. Gently stir in the prawns and clams (if using) and heat through for a further 3–4 minutes. Taste and season again.
5. Just before serving, sprinkle the soup with chopped fresh parsley, if you like.

Points per serving: 3½
Total Points per recipe: 14

Garlic and Butter Bean Soup

Serves 4

Preparation time: 10 minutes
Cooking time: 25 minutes
Calories per serving: 155; with garlic toasts 235

Freezing: not recommended

The perfect welcome-in-from-the-cold on a wintry day! Serve with Garlic Toasts (page 19).

- ½ tablespoon olive oil
- 3 garlic cloves, crushed
- 240 g (8 oz) sliced frozen cabbage
- 2 × 420 g can of butter beans, drained and rinsed
- 2 teaspoons dried herbes de Provence
- 900 ml (1½ pints) vegetable stock
- 2 tablespoons coarse-grain mustard
- fresh thyme, to garnish (optional)

1. In a large saucepan, heat the oil. Add the garlic and cabbage and fry for 4 minutes, stirring frequently.
2. Add the butter beans, herbs and stock. Season well. Simmer the soup for 25 minutes, adding extra stock if necessary.
3. Just before serving, stir in the mustard and taste to check the seasoning. Then ladle the soup into warm soup bowls and garnish with fresh thyme leaves, if you like.

Points per serving: 2; with Garlic Toasts 3½
Total Points per recipe: 8; with Garlic Toasts 14

Potato, Bacon and Apple Hot-Pot

Serves 4

Preparation and cooking time: 25 minutes
Calories per serving: 270

Freezing: not recommended

Wow, that's tasty! Even better with a crisp green salad.

- 4 rashers of lean smoked back bacon, diced
- 2 garlic cloves, crushed
- 720 g (1½ lb) potatoes, peeled and diced
- 2 teaspoons ground turmeric
- 1 teaspoon garam masala
- 1 bay leaf
- ½ teaspoon ground nutmeg
- 2 eating apples, cored and sliced thinly
- 900 ml (1½ pints) vegetable stock
- 2 tablespoons chopped fresh flat-leaf parsley (optional)
- salt and freshly ground black pepper

1. In a large saucepan, dry-fry the bacon until lightly coloured. Stir in the garlic, potatoes, turmeric, garam masala, bay leaf and nutmeg. Cook for a further 2 minutes.
2. Add the sliced apples and stock and season well. Bring to the boil and simmer for 15–20 minutes or until the potatoes are just tender. Season again to taste.
3. Ladle the hot-pot into deep soup bowls and scatter over the parsley, if you like. Serve at once.

Points per serving: 4
Total Points per recipe: 16

Scotch Broth

Serves 4

Preparation time: 10 minutes
Cooking time: 50 minutes
Calories per serving: 200

Freezing: not recommended

This Scotch Broth is so hearty it is almost a stew. Serve with warm Granary bread. To speed things up, try using dried pasta or uncooked brown rice to thicken the broth.

3 rashers of lean back bacon, diced
454 g frozen mixed casserole vegetables
120 g (4 oz) pearl barley
1 garlic clove, crushed (optional)
2 teaspoons dried thyme
1 bay leaf
grated zest of 1 lemon
1.2 litres (2 pints) vegetable stock
180 g (6 oz) frozen string beans
salt and freshly ground black pepper

1. In a large saucepan, dry-fry the bacon and frozen vegetables for a few minutes. Then cover with a lid, reduce the heat and cook for a further 2 minutes to soften.
2. Add the pearl barley, garlic, thyme, bay leaf, lemon zest and stock and season well.
3. Bring to the boil and simmer for approximately 45–50 minutes or until the barley is tender (adding extra liquid if necessary). Five minutes before the end of the cooking time, add the string beans.

Points per serving: 3
Total Points per recipe: 12

De Luxe Pasta Râgout

Serves 4

Preparation and cooking time: 35 minutes
Calories per serving: 345; with chicken 335; without meat 280

Freezing: not recommended

This chunky râgout makes a really satisfying meal. If you wish, you can leave out the meat or use 120 g (4 oz) diced chicken instead. The Points per serving will be 5, if using chicken. Without any meat at all, the Points will be 4½.

½ tablespoon olive oil
1 onion, chopped
1 garlic clove, crushed
120 g (4 oz) lean back bacon, chopped
2 celery sticks, chopped
½ teaspoon dried thyme
15 g (½ oz) plain flour
400 g can of chopped tomatoes
about 1.2 litres (2 pints) vegetable stock
120 g (4 oz) pasta shapes
420 g can of kidney beans, drained
180 g (6 oz) frozen green or runner beans
freshly ground black pepper
2 tablespoons pesto, to serve

1. Heat the oil in a pan and add the onion and garlic. Cover with a lid and cook gently for 2 minutes. Remove the lid and stir in the bacon, celery and thyme. Cover again and cook for 3 minutes.
2. Sprinkle over the flour and add the chopped tomatoes, stock and pepper. Bring to the boil and simmer gently for 20 minutes.
3. Add the pasta shapes, kidney beans and green or runner beans. Cook for a further 10–15 minutes, adding extra stock if needed. Meanwhile, dilute the pesto with a little cold water.
4. Ladle the râgout into large soup bowls and top with a whirl of the pesto. Serve at once.

Points per serving: 7
Total Points per recipe: 28

Parsnip and Pepper Goulash with Dumplings

Serves 4

Preparation time: 10 minutes
Cooking time: 50 minutes
Calories per serving: 530

Freezing: not recommended

These delicious and comforting dumplings turn simple goulash into a wonderful winter warmer.

For the goulash:
1 large onion, chopped
1 garlic clove, crushed
240 g (8 oz) frozen sliced peppers
1/2 tablespoon sunflower oil
960 g (2 lb) parsnips, peeled and chopped coarsely
2 tablespoons paprika
2 teaspoons plain flour
400 g can of chopped tomatoes
1 tablespoon tomato purée
900 ml (1 1/2 pints) vegetable stock
2 teaspoons dried thyme
1 bay leaf
freshly ground black pepper

For the herb dumplings:
120 g (4 oz) self-raising flour
60 g (2 oz) porridge oats
60 g (2 oz) polyunsaturated margarine
60 g (2 oz) reduced-fat mature Cheddar cheese, grated
1 tablespoon chopped fresh parsley
freshly ground black pepper

1. In a large saucepan or frying-pan, fry the onion, garlic and peppers in the oil until golden.
2. Add the parsnips and paprika, sprinkle over the flour and cook for a further minute, before adding the remaining ingredients for the goulash. Cover and simmer very gently for 50 minutes.
3. Meanwhile, place the flour and oats in a bowl and rub in the margarine. Add the cheese and parsley and season well with black pepper. Add enough cold water (about 120 ml/4 fl oz) to make a smooth dough and divide into 12 dumplings.
4. About 10 minutes before the end of the cooking time, pop the dumplings into the goulash so that they float on top. Replace the lid and simmer for the remaining 10 minutes. Serve immediately.

Points per serving: 8 1/2
Total Points per recipe: 34

Mexican-Style Bean Stew

Serves 4

Preparation and cooking time: 20 minutes
Calories per serving: 345; without avocado 270

Freezing: not recommended

This hot and spicy stew will certainly tingle your taste buds. Serve with a basket of tortilla chips and add 2 Points for every 30 g (1 oz) of chips.

1 tablespoon sunflower oil
1 large onion, chopped
400 g can of pimientos, drained, rinsed and sliced
2 teaspoons dried oregano
2 teaspoons ground coriander
1 garlic clove, crushed
2 × 400 g can of black-eyed beans, drained and rinsed
500 g carton of creamed tomatoes
400 g can of cherry tomatoes
3 teaspoons Tabasco sauce or to taste
a pinch of sugar
salt and freshly ground black pepper

For the topping:
1 medium ripe avocado (optional)
juice of 1 lemon (optional)
4 tablespoons low-fat natural yogurt

1. In a saucepan or small wok, heat the oil and fry the onion until softened. Add the pimientos, oregano, coriander and garlic. Cook for a further minute.
2. Stir in the beans, tomatoes, Tabasco sauce and sugar. Season well. Simmer for 15 minutes, adding a little extra water if necessary.
3. Meanwhile, stone, peel and dice the avocado, if using. Toss in the lemon juice. Season with black pepper.
4. When the stew is cooked, season again to taste and ladle into large soup bowls. Spoon a dollop of yogurt on to each bowl and top with some diced avocado, if you like.

Points per serving: 5 1/2; without avocado 4 1/2
Total Points per recipe: 22; without avocado 18

Thai-Style Soup

Serves 4

Preparation and cooking time: 20 minutes
Calories per serving: 145

Freezing: not recommended

This soup is a meal in itself!

For the stock:
1 onion, sliced finely
2 frozen skinless, boneless chicken breasts, thawed and cut into fine strips
1.2 litres (2 pints) water
grated zest of 2 lemons
1 bay leaf
2 teaspoons ginger purée
1 garlic clove, crushed
3 tablespoons light soy sauce
2 teaspoons unsweetened desiccated coconut

For the soup:
1 large carrot, cut into fine strips
chilli sauce, to taste
60 g (2 oz) rice noodles or thin egg noodles
salt and freshly ground black pepper

1. Place all the stock ingredients in a large saucepan, bring to the boil and simmer for 15 minutes.
2. Add all the soup ingredients to the stock and simmer for a further 5–6 minutes or until the noodles are just tender.
3. Ladle the soup into large soup bowls and serve at once.

Points per serving: 2½
Total Points per recipe: 10

Mint, Pea and Broccoli Soup

Serves 4

Preparation and cooking time: 25 minutes
Calories per serving: 150

Freezing: not recommended

A wonderful assortment of flavours and textures!

½ tablespoon olive oil
1 large onion, sliced
360 g (12 oz) frozen peas
a handful of lettuce leaves, washed and shredded
900 ml (1½ pints) vegetable or chicken stock
2 eggs, hard-boiled and chopped finely
grated zest of 1 lemon
1 teaspoon concentrated mint sauce or 2 tablespoons coarsely chopped fresh mint
180 g (6 oz) broccoli florets, cooked (optional)
salt and freshly ground black pepper

1. In a large saucepan, heat the olive oil and fry the onion until softened. Add the peas, lettuce and stock. Season well. Bring to the boil and simmer the soup for 15–20 minutes.
2. Meanwhile, mix together the chopped egg and lemon zest. Set to one side.
3. Just before serving the soup, add the mint sauce and broccoli florets and heat through for 1 minute. Ladle the soup into warmed soup bowls and scatter generously with the egg and lemon zest. Serve at once.

Points per serving: 2
Total Points per recipe: 8

Main Meal Salads

Salads just aren't what they used to be – thank goodness! Gone are the traditional few sad lettuce leaves and a chopped tomato, along with the notion that salads are just for the summer menu. Here is a great selection of innovative, exciting and absolutely delicious salads, which are very moreish and satisfying at the same time. Some are nothing less than exotic! Be sure to try the Vegetable Gado Gado, which is truly an Indonesian feast, and the Oriental Salad, a fabulous combination of Eastern flavours.

Warm Chicken Tikka Salad

Serves 4

Preparation and cooking time: 10 minutes
Calories per serving: 150; for each medium slice of Granary bread add 80

Freezing: not recommended

An unusual and interesting *salade tiède*, which simply means a warm salad. Make sure all the delicious juices from the pan are drizzled over the salad leaves. Serve with crusty Granary bread and add 1½ Points per medium slice.

4 small frozen skinless, boneless chicken breasts, thawed
4 tablespoons tikka paste
1 garlic clove, crushed
juice of ½ lemon
1 tablespoon sunflower oil
a selection of crisp salad leaves
salt and freshly ground black pepper
lemon wedges, for garnish

1. Cut the chicken into strips. Toss the strips with the tikka paste, garlic and lemon juice.
2. In a large frying-pan or wok, heat the sunflower oil. Add the coated chicken and any extra sauce. Stir-fry for 4–5 minutes over a high heat until cooked, reducing the heat if necessary. Season to taste.
3. Meanwhile, wash and prepare the salad leaves and divide them between 4 large plates.
4. Spoon the chicken and pan juices over the salad leaves and garnish each plate with a lemon wedge. Serve at once.

Points per serving: 3½
Total Points per recipe: 14

Jacket Potato Salad

Serves 2

Preparation and cooking time: 10 minutes + baking potatoes
Calories per serving: 360

Freezing: not recommended

A jacket potato with a difference!

2 large jacket potatoes, baked
212 g can of pink or red salmon, drained and flaked, skin and bones discarded
4 tablespoons low-fat French dressing
2 teaspoons red or green pesto
1 apple, cored and sliced finely
a handful of lettuce leaves, torn into bite-sized pieces
salt and freshly ground black pepper

1. Cut the hot jacket potatoes in half and set aside for 2 minutes.
2. In a large mixing bowl, gently toss together the salmon, French dressing, pesto and sliced apple. Using a teaspoon, scoop the potato out of the skins. Place the skins on 2 plates.
3. Gently combine the potato with the fish mixture and the salad leaves. Season well. Pile the warm potato salad back into the potato skins and serve at once.

Points per serving: 6
Total Points per recipe: 12

Vegetable Gado Gado

Serves 4

Preparation and cooking time: 30 minutes
Calories per serving: 380

Freezing: not recommended

This recipe is based on a traditional Indonesian dish; vegetables and rice are topped with a tasty nutty dressing to create a taste sensation!

240 g (8 oz) easy-cook brown rice
180 g (6 oz) cauliflower florets
410 g can of beansprouts, rinsed
1/2 cucumber, cut into fine strips
1 large carrot, grated
2 tablespoons light soy sauce
salt and freshly ground black pepper

For the nutty dressing:
1/2 tablespoon sunflower oil
1 onion, chopped finely
1 garlic clove, crushed
1 teaspoon chilli sauce or powder
1 teaspoon desiccated coconut
60 g (2 oz) cashew nuts, toasted
1 tablespoon soy sauce
150 ml (1/4 pint) water
salt and freshly ground black pepper

1. Cook the rice according to the packet instructions. Cook the cauliflower florets until just tender and then cool under running water. Set to one side to drain.
2. Meanwhile, make the dressing. In a saucepan, heat the sunflower oil and fry the onion and garlic until softened. Add all the remaining dressing ingredients and mix well. Simmer for 1 minute. Transfer the dressing to a food processor and whizz briefly. Season to taste.
3. In a large bowl, combine the vegetables and salad ingredients. Season well. Drain the rice and season with the light soy sauce.
4. To serve, spoon a mound of rice on to the centre of each plate, surround the rice with the vegetables and salad ingredients, and trickle over the warm dressing. Serve at once.

Points per serving: 5 1/2
Total Points per recipe: 22

Salade Niçoise with Salmon

Serves 4

Preparation and cooking time: 25 minutes
Calories per serving: 365

Freezing: not recommended

The old favourite with a new ingredient – a refreshingly delicious change!

- 540 g can of unpeeled new potatoes, drained and rinsed (cut in half if large)
- 1 tablespoon olive oil
- 2 tablespoons soy sauce
- 1 large onion, sliced finely
- 2 handfuls of crisp lettuce leaves, torn into bite-sized pieces
- 2 large tomatoes, chopped roughly
- 2 hard-boiled eggs, quartered
- 400 g can of red salmon, drained and flaked roughly, skin and bones discarded
- 240 g (8 oz) whole frozen green beans, cooked and cooled under cold water
- 3 tablespoons low-fat French dressing
- salt and freshly ground black pepper

1. Preheat the oven to Gas Mark 6/200°C/400°F.
2. Place the potatoes in a small roasting tin. Toss in the olive oil, soy sauce and onion. Season well with black pepper. Roast in the oven for 15 minutes.
3. Meanwhile, in a large salad bowl or platter (or 4 individual serving plates), arrange the lettuce and scatter over the tomatoes, hard-boiled eggs and salmon. Season well.
4. Just before serving, remove the potatoes from the oven and mix them with the whole green beans and French dressing. Spoon the dressed potatoes and beans over the salad and serve at once.

Points per serving: $5^1/_2$
Total Points per recipe: 22

Mediterranean Pizza Salad

Serves 6

Preparation time: 30 minutes
Cooking time: 25 minutes
Calories per serving: 280

Freezing: not recommended

This is not the usual pizza or the usual salad – it's an extraordinarily tasty combination! Feel free to experiment with any salad ingredients you have.

- low-fat cooking spray
- 2 × 145 g pizza base mix
- 2 teaspoons dried herbes de Provence
- 290 g jar of antipasto mixed peppers in tomato sauce
- 300 g can of mushrooms, drained
- 90 g (3 oz) reduced-fat mature Cheddar cheese, grated
- a combination of salad ingredients of your choice (see below)
- 3 tablespoons low-fat French dressing

1. Preheat the oven to Gas Mark 6/200°C/400°F. Lightly spray a baking tray with low-fat cooking spray.
2. Make up the pizza dough according to the packet instructions and add the herbes de Provence. Knead on a floured surface for 30 seconds.
3. Roll the dough out to a 30 cm (12-inch) round and place on the prepared baking tray. Spread the peppers over the dough and scatter with the drained mushrooms. Pinch the edges to form a rim.
4. Bake in the oven for 20–25 minutes, or until the topping is bubbling hot and the base just crisp.
5. Meanwhile, prepare the salad ingredients for the topping and season well. Drizzle over the French dressing and toss together.
6. Remove the pizza from the oven and carefully transfer from the baking tray to a large platter or chopping board. Pile on the salad and sprinkle with the cheese. Serve at once.

Cook's note:
Some suggested salad ingredients are sliced iceberg, chopped ripe tomatoes, watercress and radishes.

Points per serving: 3
Total Points per recipe: 18

Oriental Salad

Serves 4

Preparation and cooking time: 15 minutes
Calories per serving: 540

Freezing: not recommended

Cold noodles may sound odd, however tossed in this dressing they're a taste sensation!

240 g pack of fine egg noodles
2 carrots, sliced very thinly on a slant
180 g (6 oz) frozen peas, cooked and cooled
227 g can of water chestnuts, sliced finely
4 slices of lean ham, cut into fine strips (optional)
1 tablespoon toasted sesame seeds
salt and freshly ground black pepper
For the dressing:
2 tablespoons white wine vinegar
3 tablespoons soy sauce
2 teaspoons sesame oil
2 tablespoons sunflower oil
2 garlic cloves, crushed
1 teaspoon ground coriander
2.5 cm (1-inch) piece of fresh root ginger, chopped; or 2 teaspoons ginger purée
freshly ground black pepper

1. Cook the noodles according to the packet instructions. Drain the noodles and rinse quickly under cold running water. Drain well.
2. In a liquidiser or screw-top jar, blend all the dressing ingredients together.
3. Turn the noodles into a large serving bowl, pour over the dressing and toss well. Add the remaining salad ingredients and toss again. Season to taste and serve cold.

Cook's note:
Fresh root ginger can be grated and stored in the freezer.

Points per serving: 6½
Total Points per recipe: 26

Borlotti Salad

Serves 4

Preparation and cooking time: 10 minutes
Calories per serving: 230; for each medium slice of toast add 80

Freezing: not recommended

Delicious with crisp salad leaves and Granary toast. Add 1½ Points per medium slice of toast.

420 g (14 oz) can of borlotti beans, drained and rinsed
420 g (14 oz) can of green lentils, drained and rinsed
For the dressing:
1 large onion, sliced finely
2 bay leaves, crumbled
2 large tomatoes, chopped
1 tablespoon red wine vinegar
1 tablespoon olive oil
juice and zest of 1 lemon
salt and freshly ground black pepper

1. In a bowl, mix together the onion, bay leaves, tomatoes, wine vinegar, olive oil, lemon juice and zest. Season well. Turn into a saucepan and heat gently for 2 minutes.
2. Add the drained beans and lentils to the saucepan and toss well, until coated in the dressing. If possible, leave to stand for 20 minutes before serving, to allow the flavours to develop.

Points per serving: 6½
Total Points per recipe: 26½

Feasts from the Sea

You can whip up an ocean of dishes with canned, smoked, fresh or frozen fish – the possibilities are endless! Seafood is so tasty and so good for you: treat yourself and your family to healthy meals such as Teriyaki Tuna Steak with Ginger and Garlic or Linguine with Peppers and Clams. Go ahead, dive in and enjoy!

Crab Cakes with Spicy Cucumber Relish

Makes 12 cakes

Preparation and cooking time: 10 minutes + 8 minutes grilling
Calories per cake: 130; with mackerel 140

Freezing: not recommended

The combination of crab and Thai flavours works wonders. Serve with a crisp salad, cucumber relish and hot black bean sauce.

60 g (2 oz) polyunsaturated margarine
60 g (2 oz) plain flour, plus extra for shaping
120 ml (4 fl oz) skimmed milk
90 g jar of red Thai curry paste
1 large onion, chopped finely
2 × 170 g can of crabmeat in brine, drained
120 g (4 oz) fresh white breadcrumbs
sunflower oil, for brushing

For the spicy cucumber relish:
½ cucumber, chopped finely
2 tomatoes, chopped finely
1 small onion, chopped finely
green or red Tabasco sauce, to taste
salt and freshly ground black pepper

For the hot black bean sauce:
160 g jar of black bean sauce
60 ml (2 fl oz) water
salt and freshly ground black pepper

1. In a small saucepan, melt the margarine and then add the flour and cook for 1 minute. Remove from the heat, pour in the milk and beat until smooth. Return the pan to the heat and cook for a further 2 minutes, stirring frequently. Pile the thick sauce on to a plate and spread out to allow to cool.
2. In a large mixing bowl, mix together the cooled thick sauce, Thai curry paste, onion, crabmeat and breadcrumbs until well combined.
3. Using floured hands, divide the mixture into 12 pieces and shape each one into a 5 cm (2-inch) patty. Chill until required.
4. Preheat the grill to a medium heat. In a bowl, combine all the cucumber relish ingredients and season to taste.
5. Place the crab cakes on a non-stick baking tray and lightly brush each side of the cakes with a little sunflower oil. Grill the crab cakes for 3–4 minutes each side.
6. Meanwhile, heat the black bean sauce with the water and season.
7. Serve the crab cakes surrounded with crisp lettuce leaves. Serve the relish and sauce separately.

Cook's note:
Canned mackerel can be used in place of the crab. The Points per cake will be 4½.

Points per cake: 3½
Total Points per recipe: 42

Grilled Salmon Fillets

Serves 4

Preparation and cooking time: 15 minutes
Calories per serving: 290

Freezing: not recommended

Serve these with the Low-Fat Chips (right) so you can enjoy fish and chips absolutely guilt-free.

4 thick 150 g (5 oz) pieces of salmon fillet
2 teaspoons olive oil
Herb and spice mix:
½ teaspoon cayenne pepper
½ teaspoon dried thyme
½ teaspoon dried basil
½ teaspoon dried oregano
3 teaspoons paprika
salt and freshly ground black pepper

1. Brush the flesh side of the salmon with a teaspoon of the olive oil.
2. Preheat the grill to a medium setting.
3. Mix together the herbs and spices and coat the flesh side of the salmon fillets.
4. Heat a frying-pan with a teaspoon of olive oil, until very hot. Lay the salmon fillets, flesh-side down, in the pan and cook over a medium heat until very brown (about 1 or 2 minutes).
5. Remove the pan from the heat and place under the grill (making sure the pan handle is facing out). Grill for approximately 5–7 minutes or until the skin is golden brown and the fish is cooked.
6. Remove from the grill, turn the fish over and serve the salmon fillets, flesh-side up.

Points per serving: 4½
Total Points per recipe: 18

Low-Fat Chips

Serves 4

Preparation time: 5 minutes
Cooking time: 40 minutes
Calories per serving: 235

Freezing: not recommended

Simple, but oh-so-tasty!

720 g (1½ lb) medium potatoes
2 tablespoons sunflower or olive oil
3 tablespoons light soy sauce
salt and freshly ground black pepper

1. Preheat the oven to Gas Mark 6/200°C/400°F.
2. Scrub clean the potatoes and cut into thick chips.
3. Place in a large roasting tin and toss in the oil and light soy sauce. Season with the salt and pepper. Bake for 30–40 minutes, turning occasionally, until golden and crisp.

Points per serving: 3½
Total Points per recipe: 14

Smoked Haddock in Filo Pastry

Serves 4

Preparation time: 15 minutes
Cooking time: 45 minutes
Calories per serving: 305

Freezing: not recommended

Take advantage of the wide range of delicious, ready-made tomato sauces and whip this fish pie up in minutes.

360 g (12 oz) frozen leaf spinach
1 garlic clove, crushed
1/2 teaspoon ground nutmeg
2 × 300 g can of button mushrooms in brine, drained
720 g (1 1/2 lb) frozen skinless smoked haddock fillets
350 g jar of ready-made, flavoured tomato sauce
4 sheets of filo pastry
milk and beaten egg, for brushing
1 tablespoon sesame seeds
salt and freshly ground black pepper

1. Preheat the oven to Gas Mark 6/200°C/400°F.
2. In a large saucepan, cook the spinach over a moderate heat to evaporate the water, add the garlic and nutmeg and season well. Spread the spinach mix into a large, shallow gratin dish (about 1.2–1.7 litres/2–3 pints), and allow to cool.
3. Spoon the mushrooms evenly over the top of the spinach and lay the haddock fillets evenly over the mushrooms. Finish with an even layer of pasta sauce.
4. Lay one filo pastry sheet over the pie mix and brush with milk. Continue this with a further 3 sheets of filo pastry, brushing the top of the final sheet with beaten egg.
5. With a sharp knife, lightly slash the top of the pastry in a lattice pattern. Scatter over the sesame seeds and bake for 40–45 minutes until piping hot and golden brown.

Points per serving: 3
Total Points per recipe: 12

Fish and String Bean Korma

Serves 4

Preparation and cooking time: 20 minutes
Calories per serving: 225; with boiled rice 535

Freezing: not recommended

Perfect with flavoured basmati rice or plain boiled rice. Add 3 Points for each medium serving.

1/2 tablespoon sunflower oil
1 large onion, chopped
1 bay leaf
2 teaspoons ground turmeric
1 tablespoon mild curry powder
1 tablespoon desiccated unsweetened coconut
450 ml (3/4 pint) vegetable stock
180 g (6 oz) frozen runner beans
480 g (1 lb) frozen cod, thawed and cut into 4 cm (1 1/2-inch) cubes
120 g (4 oz) curd cheese
salt and freshly ground black pepper
roughly chopped fresh coriander, to garnish (optional)

1. In a large frying-pan or wok, heat the oil and fry the onion until softened.
2. Add the bay leaf, turmeric, curry powder and coconut. Cook over a gentle heat for 2 minutes. Pour in the stock and simmer for 3–4 minutes.
3. Add the runner beans and simmer for a further 2 minutes, then add the fish pieces and season. Cover and cook gently for 2 minutes or until the fish is just cooked.
4. Meanwhile, mix the curd cheese with a little water, to reach the consistency of double cream. Pour the curd cheese into the pan, and gently mix through until piping hot. Scatter over the coriander, if you like, and serve at once.

Points per serving: 3 1/2
Total Points per recipe: 14

Pasta Paella

Serves 4

Preparation and cooking time: 20 minutes
Calories per serving: 495

Freezing: not recommended

When we think of paella, rice immediately springs to mind. Here's a Spanish variation using pasta, for a much lighter texture.

1 tablespoon olive oil
1 large onion, chopped
4 garlic cloves, crushed
1 bay leaf
2 teaspoons ground turmeric
360 g (12 oz) dried pasta shapes (twists or shells)
1.2 litres (2 pints) vegetable stock
2 large carrots
360 g (12 oz) broccoli florets
240 g (8 oz) large, frozen cooked prawns, peeled
salt and freshly ground black pepper

1. In a large frying-pan or wok, heat the oil and fry the onion with the garlic, until softened and coloured.
2. Add the bay leaf, turmeric, pasta and half the vegetable stock. Season well. Cover and simmer for 5 minutes.
3. With a vegetable peeler (a swivel peeler is best), peel the carrots into ribbon-like strips and set to one side.
4. Remove the lid from the pan, stir in the broccoli florets and simmer for 4 minutes, adding extra stock if the pan becomes too dry.
5. Add the prawns and carrot ribbons and simmer for a final 2 minutes or until the prawns are piping hot. Season to taste and transfer to a serving dish.

Points per serving: 5
Total Points per recipe: 20

Ocean Pizza Pie

Serves 6

Preparation time: 20 minutes
Cooking time: 30 minutes
Calories per serving: 330

Freezing: not recommended

Ideal for pizza and seafood lovers alike.

low-fat cooking spray
2 × 145 g packet of pizza dough mix
2 garlic cloves, crushed
1 tablespoon dried oregano
250 g jar of tomato sauce pizza topping
400 g can of kidney beans, drained and rinsed
Tabasco sauce, to taste
400 g can of tuna fish in brine, drained and flaked
1 large onion, sliced thinly
90 g (3 oz) low-fat mature Cheddar cheese, grated
freshly ground black pepper

1. Preheat the oven to Gas Mark 6/200°C/400°F. Lightly spray a non-stick baking tray.
2. Make the pizza dough according to the packet instructions, adding the garlic and oregano to the mixture.
3. Roll out the pizza dough into a 30 cm (12-inch) round and place on the baking tray.
4. In a bowl, combine the tomato sauce with the kidney beans and add the Tabasco sauce to taste. Spread this over the pizza base, followed by the flaked tuna, and scatter over the sliced onion and cheese.
5. Season well with black pepper and bake the pizza for 25–30 minutes or until cooked and bubbling hot.

Points per serving: 5
Total Points per recipe: 30

Quick Salmon Kedgeree

Serves 4

Preparation and cooking time: 15 minutes
Calories per serving: 580

Freezing: not recommended

Kedgeree originates from an Indian dish, which the Victorians discovered and then adapted to their own tastes. This recipe is quick to make and a good use for canned salmon.

1 large onion, chopped
1/2 tablespoon olive oil
1 tablespoon garam masala
juice and zest of 1 lemon
120 g (4 oz) frozen petits pois
60 g (2 oz) sultanas
418 g can of red salmon in brine, drained, juice reserved and flaked, skin and bones removed
2 × 277 g can of brown rice
4 hard-boiled eggs, chopped roughly
2 tablespoons roughly chopped fresh parsley
salt and freshly ground black pepper
lemon wedges, to serve

1. In a large frying-pan or wok, gently cook the onion in the olive oil, until softened but not coloured.
2. Add the garam masala and fry for 30 seconds. Then add the lemon juice and zest, 150 ml (1/4 pint) water, petits pois, sultanas and reserved salmon juice. Bring the contents of the pan to the boil and simmer for 2–3 minutes or until the liquid is reduced by half.
3. Add the rice and heat through for 2 minutes, stirring frequently.
4. Gently fold in the flaked salmon, eggs and parsley. Season to taste and heat through until piping hot. Serve at once, with the lemon wedges.

Points per serving: 7
Total Points per recipe: 28

Roasted Haddock with Herbs

Serves 4

Preparation time: 5 minutes
Cooking time: 15 minutes
Calories per serving: 250

Freezing: not recommended

Enjoy the clean and refreshing taste of baked fish with herbs and mustard.

30 g (1 oz) fresh breadcrumbs
2 teaspoons herbes de Provence
2 tablespoons roughly chopped fresh parsley (optional)
60 g (2 oz) low-fat Cheddar cheese, grated
4 tablespoons coarse-grain mustard
4 × 180 g (6 oz) frozen haddock or cod steak portions, thawed
salt and freshly ground black pepper
lemon or orange wedges, to serve

1. Preheat the oven to Gas Mark 6/200°C/400°F.
2. In a mixing bowl, stir together the breadcrumbs, herbs, parsley (if using), and cheese. Season well.
3. Spread the mustard evenly over one side of the fish steaks and place in a shallow, ovenproof dish. Divide the crumb mixture between the fish steaks and press the crumbs gently into the mustard.
4. Bake in the oven for 12–15 minutes, or until the fish is just cooked and golden brown. Serve with the lemon or orange wedges.

Points per serving: 3 1/2
Total Points per recipe: 14

Salmon Muffins with Dill Sauce

Makes 8 muffins

Preparation and cooking time: 20 minutes
Calories per muffin: 100

Freezing: not recommended

Absolutely scrumptious!

low-fat cooking spray
150 g (5 oz) self-raising flour
1 teaspoon bicarbonate of soda
418 g can of pink salmon, drained and flaked, skin and bones removed
120 ml (4 fl oz) low-fat natural yogurt
1 egg, beaten
½ tablespoon olive oil
1 tablespoon red Thai curry paste or 1 teaspoon chilli powder
paprika, to decorate
green salad leaves, to serve

For the dill sauce:
½ cucumber, grated
300 ml (½ pint) low-fat natural yogurt
60 g (2 oz) low-fat soft cheese
1 teaspoon lemon juice
2 teaspoons dill weed
salt and freshly ground black pepper

1. Preheat the oven to Gas Mark 7/220°C/425°F. Lightly spray a large muffin or patty tin with low-fat cooking spray.
2. Sift the flour and bicarbonate of soda into a large mixing bowl. Stir in the flaked salmon.
3. Make a well in the centre and pour in the yogurt, egg, oil and Thai paste or chilli powder. Briefly fold all the ingredients together and season well.
4. Spoon the mixture into the prepared tins to about three-quarters full. Do not smooth the tops. Sprinkle the muffins with paprika and bake for 10–12 minutes, until risen and browned.
5. Meanwhile, combine all the ingredients together for the dill sauce. Season to taste.
6. To serve, split open the hot fish muffins and place on a serving plate of green salad leaves. Drizzle over the dill sauce and serve.

Points per muffin: 3½
Total Points per recipe: 28

Teriyaki Tuna Steaks with Ginger and Garlic

Serves 4

Preparation and cooking time: 10 minutes + 2 hours marinating
Calories per serving: 280

Freezing: not recommended

A wonderful dish for entertaining – so easy yet the flavour is so good you'll be sure to get loads of compliments.

4 × 180 g (6 oz) frozen tuna steaks
For the marinade:
4 tablespoons light soy sauce
1 tablespoon sunflower oil
2 tablespoons white wine vinegar or lemon juice
2 garlic cloves, crushed
2 teaspoons ginger purée
300 ml (1/2 pint) orange juice
salt and freshly ground black pepper

1. In a large bowl, mix together all the marinade ingredients and season well.
2. Lay the tuna steaks in the marinade and marinate for 2 hours, or until the steaks have thawed completely.
3. Preheat the grill to a medium setting.
4. Remove the tuna from the marinade and place the fish on a non-stick baking tray. Spoon over half of the remaining marinade. Grill for approximately 3 minutes each side, basting with the marinade as the tuna cooks.

Points per serving: 4
Total Points per recipe: 16

Linguine with Peppers and Clams

Serves 4

Preparation and cooking time: 15 minutes
Calories per serving: 480

Freezing: not recommended

You'll love the combinations of peppers and clams and the delicious gravy-like sauce.

360 g (12 oz) dried linguine, spaghetti or vermicelli
1 large onion, sliced
1/2 tablespoon olive oil
480 g (1 lb) frozen sliced peppers
1 small glass of dry white wine
150 ml (1/4 pint) vegetable stock
290 g can of clams, drained
120 g (4 oz) frozen peas
1 tablespoon green pesto
salt and freshly ground black pepper

1. Cook the pasta in plenty of boiling, salted water until *al dente* or just cooked.
2. Meanwhile, in a large frying-pan, cook the onion in the olive oil until softened and slightly coloured.
3. Add the peppers and cook for a further 2 minutes. Then add the white wine and the stock. Stir in the clams and the frozen peas. Cover the pan and simmer for 2 minutes.
4. Meanwhile, drain the pasta. Stir the pesto sauce into the clam and pepper sauce and season well.
5. Tip the drained pasta into a large, warm serving dish and toss quickly with the sauce. Serve at once.

Points per serving: 5 1/2
Total Points per recipe: 22

Main Courses

In this chapter, you'll find both vegetarian and meat dishes. But these are meat dishes with a difference: the meat is a flavouring and not the main ingredient. Not only will this take the strain off your purse strings but it will be much easier on your waistline; so make more of pasta, vegetables and grains. Warming meals such as Bubble and Squeak with Mushroom Râgout are sure to be a favourite with the family and the Lentil *Sag* with Raisin and Mint Raita will be a refreshing change on the midweek menu.

Chicken with Orange and Dill

Serves 4

Preparation and cooking time: 20 minutes + marinating
Calories per serving: 175

Freezing: not recommended

Frozen turkey steaks could be used instead of the chicken breasts and the Points will remain the same. Serve with a mixed salad and new potatoes, adding 1 Point per medium potato.

4 small, frozen, boneless, skinless chicken breasts, thawed

For the marinade

grated zest and juice of 2 oranges
1 tablespoon olive oil
1 garlic clove, crushed
2 teaspoons dried dill
1 tablespoon runny honey
salt and freshly ground black pepper

1. Place the chicken breasts between two sheets of cling film and lightly beat with a rolling pin, until almost doubled in size.
2. In a mixing bowl, combine all the marinade ingredients.
3. Place the chicken escalopes in the marinade, cover and refrigerate for at least 30 minutes, or overnight.
4. Preheat the grill to a moderate setting.
5. Lay the chicken escalopes on a baking tray and grill for 5–7 minutes on each side or until the chicken is cooked through. Baste the escalopes as they cook with the remaining marinade.
6. Serve at once, with the grill-pan juices.

Points per serving: 3½
Total Points per recipe: 14

Tomato, Red Pepper and Spinach Pies

Serves 4

Preparation time: 15 minutes
Cooking time: 20 minutes
Calories per serving: 210

Freezing: not recommended

Simple yet very stylish.

145 g packet of pizza dough mix
2 teaspoons dried oregano
240 g (8 oz) frozen chopped spinach
1 teaspoon ground nutmeg
400 g can of cherry tomatoes, drained
270 g jar of sliced mixed peppers, drained
30 g (1 oz) Parmesan cheese, grated
salt and freshly ground black pepper

1. Preheat the oven to Gas Mark 6/200°C/400°F.
2. Prepare the dough according to the packet instructions, adding the dried oregano.
3. In a frying-pan, dry-fry the spinach until thawed and the excess water has evaporated. Remove from the heat and season with the nutmeg, salt and pepper.
4. Divide the dough equally into 4. On a floured surface, roll each piece into a circle about 15–18 cm (6–7 inches) in diameter. Transfer to a non-stick baking tray.
5. Spread each pastry base with the spinach, leaving a 2.5 cm (1-inch) border. Arrange the cherry tomatoes and sliced peppers on top. Fold and turn up the pastry edges to form a rough edge.
6. Sprinkle each tart with some grated Parmesan and bake for 15–20 minutes until cooked and golden.

Points per serving: 3
Total Points per recipe: 12

Bubble and Squeak with Mushroom Râgout

Serves 4

Preparation and cooking time: 20 minutes
Calories per serving: 320

Freezing: not recommended

The term 'bubble and squeak' describes the bubbling of potatoes and cabbage as they boil in water and the subsequent squeaking in the frying-pan. In this version, there's no squeak but plenty of flavour.

720 g (1½ lb) potatoes, scrubbed and cut into even-sized chunks
1 tablespoon sunflower oil
1 large onion, sliced
480 g (1 lb) frozen button mushrooms
150 ml (¼ pint) white wine or vegetable stock
1 bay leaf
240 g (8 oz) frozen shredded cabbage
1 teaspoon ground nutmeg
2 tablespoons semi-skimmed milk
3 tablespoons coarse-grain mustard
200 g tub of low-fat fromage frais
2 tablespoons chopped fresh parsley (optional)
salt and freshly ground black pepper

1. Boil the potatoes in a large saucepan.
2. In a large frying-pan, heat half the oil and fry the onion until softened and lightly coloured.
3. Stir in the mushrooms and fry over a high heat for 3–4 minutes. Add the wine, or stock, and bay leaf and season well. Simmer for 3 minutes and remove from the heat.
4. Stir-fry the cabbage in the remaining oil until heated through and season well with the nutmeg, salt and pepper.
5. Drain and mash the cooked potato. Mix in the cabbage, adding a little milk if the mixture is too stiff. Season to taste and keep warm.
6. Return the mushrooms to the heat and stir in the mustard. When bubbling hot, remove from the heat and stir in the fromage frais.
7. To serve, spoon the mushroom râgout into 4 large soup bowls and top with a generous mound of bubble. Scatter with fresh parsley if you wish.

Points per serving: 4
Total Points per recipe: 16

Stir-Fry Teriyaki Vegetables

Serves 4

Preparation and cooking time: 15 minutes
Calories per serving: 600

Freezing: not recommended

Rice is the best accompaniment to this dish; however, noodles are a good alternative.

360 g (12 oz) long-grain rice
1 tablespoon sunflower oil
180 g (6 oz) frozen broccoli florets
1 garlic clove, crushed
180 g (6 oz) frozen whole green beans
227 g can of water chestnuts, drained and sliced
425 g can of baby sweetcorn, drained and cut in half lengthways
410 g can of beansprouts, drained
½ bunch of spring onions, chopped (optional)
2 teaspoons ginger purée
150 g (5 oz) teriyaki sauce
light soy sauce
freshly ground black pepper
90 g (3 oz) cashew nuts, toasted

1. Cook the rice in plenty of boiling, salted water until just tender.
2. In a wok, heat the oil and stir-fry the frozen broccoli and garlic for 2–3 minutes, then add the frozen whole green beans and continue to stir-fry for a further minute.
3. Add the remaining vegetables and ginger. Cook for a further 2 minutes.
4. Pour in the teriyaki sauce and carefully toss through the vegetables. Cook for a further minute, or until heated through, and season to taste.
5. Drain the rice and spoon a mound into the centre of each of 4 large dinner plates. Sprinkle over a little soy sauce and black pepper. Spoon the vegetables around the rice and scatter over the cashew nuts. Serve at once.

Points per serving: 8½
Total Points per recipe: 34

Pasta Bows with Apples and Bacon

Serves 4

Preparation and cooking time: 25 minutes
Calories per serving: 490
Freezing: not recommended

These pasta bows are truly delicious.

360 g (12 oz) dried pasta bows
4 rashers of lean smoked bacon, diced
2 leeks, chopped
1 garlic clove, crushed
2 eating apples, cored and sliced
400 g can of chopped tomatoes
500 g carton of creamed tomatoes
150 ml (1/4 pint) vegetable stock
1 bay leaf
120 g (4 oz) frozen petits pois
salt and freshly ground black pepper

1. In a large saucepan of water, cook the pasta until *al dente,* or just tender.
2. Meanwhile, in a frying-pan, dry-fry the bacon and leeks until lightly coloured.
3. Stir in the garlic, apples, tomatoes, creamed tomatoes, stock and bay leaf. Season well.
4. Simmer the sauce for 15 minutes, adding the petits pois for the final 3 minutes of cooking.
5. Drain the pasta and divide into 4 large soup bowls or plates. Ladle over the sauce and serve.

Points per serving: 6
Total Points per recipe: 24

Meat Patties with Bulgar Wheat and Salsa

Serves 4

Preparation time: 20 minutes standing + 30 minutes chilling
Cooking time: 20 minutes
Calories per serving: 605

Freezing: not recommended

Minced lamb, pork or beef can be used in this recipe. With pork, the Points will be the same as the beef; with lamb and salsa, the Points per serving will be 6 1/2, with lamb and blue cheese they will be 7.

240 g (8 oz) bulgar wheat
240 g (8 oz) extra-lean frozen minced beef, thawed
1 large onion, grated
2 garlic cloves, crushed
2 tablespoons Worcestershire sauce
1 egg, beaten
salt and freshly ground black pepper
To serve:
4 medium pitta breads
226 g jar of hot chilli tomato salsa or 170 g carton of low-fat blue cheese dressing
a selection of salad leaves

1. In a large bowl, cover the bulgar wheat with 600 ml (1 pint) of boiling water and leave to stand for 20 minutes.
2. Preheat the oven to Gas Mark 6/200°C/400°F.
3. Drain the bulgar wheat thoroughly, by squeezing it in a clean tea towel to extract as much of the water as possible. Then spread it out to cool on a large plate.
4. Meanwhile, in a large bowl, mix together the mince, onion, garlic, Worcestershire sauce and egg. Season well.
5. Add the cooled bulgar wheat. Using your hands, form the mixture into 8 round patties and place on a non-stick baking tray. Chill for at least 30 minutes.
6. Bake the meat patties for 15–20 minutes or until cooked.
7. To serve, warm the pitta breads, then split and fill each with salad leaves, a meat patty and a splash of salsa or dressing.

Points per serving: with salsa 6; with blue cheese 7 1/2
Total Points per recipe: with salsa 24; with blue cheese 30

Lentil *Sag*

Serves 4

Preparation and cooking time: 25 minutes
Calories per serving: 445; with boiled rice 755

Freezing: not recommended

A *Sag* is an Indian-style dish containing spinach. Serve with rice (either basmati or plain long-grain) and add 3 Points for a medium serving. You should also accompany this dish with the Raisin and Mint Raita (see opposite), adding 2 Points per serving.

1 tablespoon sunflower oil
1 large onion, chopped
4 garlic cloves, crushed
1 tablespoon ground turmeric
1 tablespoon garam masala
6 cardamom pods, crushed
1 bay leaf
480 g (1 lb) red lentils, washed
about 1 litre (1³/₄ pints) vegetable stock
240 g (8 oz) chopped frozen spinach

1. In a large saucepan, heat the oil and fry the onion until golden brown.
2. Stir in the garlic and spices and fry gently for 1 minute, until lightly toasted.
3. Add the lentils and stock and season well. Simmer for 15–20 minutes or until the lentils are just tender, adding extra stock if the pan becomes dry.
4. Stir in the chopped spinach and cook for a further 5 minutes, stirring frequently, until the spinach is cooked. Season to taste.

Points per serving: 4
Total Points per recipe: 16

Raisin and Mint Raita

Serves 4

Preparation time: 5 minutes
Calories per serving: 115

Freezing: not recommended

Any chopped dried fruit can be used in place of the raisins. Serve with the Lentil *Sag* (see left).

120 g (4 oz) raisins, chopped
2 teaspoons mint sauce
300 ml (¹/₂ pint) low-fat natural yogurt
2 spring onions, chopped
salt and freshly ground black pepper

1. Simply combine all the raita ingredients in a bowl. Pour into a serving dish and chill until required.

Points per serving: 2
Total Points per recipe: 8

Lamb and Herb Meatloaf

Serves 8

Preparation time: 10 minutes
Cooking time: 1 hour
Calories per serving: 405

Freezing: not recommended

A true family favourite, traditionally served with loads of gravy. Serve it with pickled red cabbage and jacket potatoes, topped with low-fat fromage frais, for an amazing taste combination. It is also excellent cold with salad.

480 g (1 lb) lean frozen minced lamb, thawed
2 garlic cloves, crushed
3 large carrots, grated
2 teaspoons ground cumin
1 teaspoon ground cinnamon
1 large onion, grated
2 tablespoons Worcestershire sauce
2 tablespoons tomato purée
180 g (6 oz) fresh breadcrumbs
2 eggs, beaten
salt and freshly ground black pepper

1. Preheat the oven to Gas Mark 5/190°C/375°F. Line a 1 kg (2 lb) loaf tin with greaseproof paper.
2. In a large bowl, thoroughly mix all the ingredients together and season well. Press the mix into the loaf tin and cover with aluminium foil.
3. Cook the loaf for approximately 1 hour, or until firm and a skewer or knife comes out clean when inserted. Allow the loaf to sit in its tin for 10 minutes before turning out and slicing.
4. Serve cut into thick slices.

Points per serving: 9½
Total Points per recipe: 38

Lentil and Mushroom Haggis

Serves 4

Preparation time: 10 minutes
Cooking time: 2 hours steaming
Calories per serving: 405

Freezing: not recommended

Barley is a good alternative to rice or potatoes. It can be cooked ahead and kept for several days in the refrigerator. It's ideal for this tasty haggis, which takes some time to steam, but can be put together in a flash.

low-fat cooking spray
1 tablespoon olive oil
1 large onion, chopped
2 large carrots, grated
2 × 300 g can of sliced mushrooms, drained
2 teaspoons dried sage
215 g can of kidney beans, drained and rinsed
420 g can of green lentils, drained and rinsed
60 g (2 oz) pearl barley, cooked
60 g (2 oz) porridge oats
2 teaspoons yeast or vegetable extract
1 egg
salt and freshly ground black pepper

For the sauce:
1 large onion, sliced
½ tablespoon olive oil
2 tablespoons orange marmalade
500 g carton of creamed tomatoes
salt and freshly ground black pepper

1. Prepare a steamer for the haggis. Lightly spray a 1-litre (1¾-pint) pudding basin with the low-fat cooking spray and line the base with a piece of greaseproof paper.
2. In a saucepan, heat the oil and gently fry the onion until golden brown. Add the carrots and mushrooms and fry for a further 3 minutes.
3. Turn this mixture into a large mixing bowl and add the rest of the haggis ingredients. Using a potato masher or fork, mash all the ingredients together and season well.
4. Put the haggis mixture into the prepared pudding basin, cover with a double layer of aluminium foil and secure with string.
5. Place in the steamer and cook for 2 hours.
6. Fifteen minutes before serving, prepare the sauce. Fry the onion in the olive oil until softened and lightly coloured. Add the marmalade and creamed tomatoes and season well. Simmer for 5 minutes.
7. To serve, remove the haggis from the steamer. Take off the foil and turn the haggis on to a serving plate. Serve the sauce separately.

Points per serving: 5
Total Points per recipe: 20

Pork and Apple Cobbler

Serves 4

Preparation time: 20 minutes
Cooking time: 25 minutes
Calories per serving: 675

Freezing: not recommended

Here meat is a flavouring rather than the main ingredient. Pork and apples are a fabulous taste combination.

2 large onions, chopped
1/2 tablespoon olive oil
240 g (8 oz) frozen minced pork, thawed
4 teaspoons plain flour
2 teaspoons dried thyme
1 bay leaf
480 g (1 lb) frozen vegetable casserole mix
600 ml (1 pint) vegetable stock
salt and freshly ground black pepper

For the topping:
240 g (8 oz) plain flour
2 1/2 teaspoons baking powder
45 g (1 1/2 oz) polyunsaturated margarine
2 medium eating apples, cored and grated
2 teaspoons dried thyme
about 150 ml (1/4 pint) skimmed milk
salt and freshly ground black pepper
milk, for brushing

1. In a non-stick saucepan, gently fry the onions in the olive oil until softened and golden brown.
2. Add the pork and toss over a high heat until browned. Sprinkle over the flour and cook for 30 seconds. Then add the thyme, bay leaf, vegetables and stock. Season well with salt and pepper.
3. Bring to the boil and simmer for 15–20 minutes.
4. Preheat the oven to Gas Mark 6/200°C/400°F.
5. For the cobbler topping, in a large bowl, sift the flour and baking powder together. Rub in the margarine with your fingertips. Then stir in the grated apple and thyme and season with salt and pepper. Add enough milk to make a soft dough.
6. On a floured surface, roll the dough out to approximately 2 cm (3/4-inch) thick and cut into 8 rounds.
7. Spoon the pork into a shallow, ovenproof dish and top with the cobbler. Brush the cobbler tops with milk and bake for 20–25 minutes or until bubbling hot.

Points per serving: 8
Total Points per recipe: 32

Mustard, Bean and Chicken Pies

Serves 6

Preparation time: 20 minutes
Cooking time: 20 minutes
Calories per serving: 400

Freezing: not recommended

Serve these filling pies warm and with plenty of crisp green salad.

For the pastry:
360 g (12 oz) plain flour
1 teaspoon baking powder
2 tablespoons dried chopped onion
2 teaspoons herbes de Provence or thyme or oregano
2 tablespoons olive oil
a pinch of salt

For the filling:
180 g (6 oz) cooked, skinless chicken, cut into strips
400 g can of ratatouille
420 g can of mixed beans in chilli sauce
2 teaspoons Dijon mustard
salt and freshly ground black pepper
paprika, for dusting

1. Preheat the oven to Gas Mark 6/200°C/400°F.
2. Sieve the flour and baking powder into a large mixing bowl. Stir in the dried onion, herbs and salt.
3. In a measuring jug, mix together 150 ml (1/4 pint) of warm water and the olive oil. Gradually add the liquid to the dry ingredients and mix to a soft dough, adding a little extra water if necessary.
4. Cover the dough and chill.
5. Meanwhile, in a large mixing bowl, combine all the filling ingredients together and season to taste.
6. Roll out the chilled pastry into 6 saucer-sized circles about 18 cm (7 inches) in diameter.
7. Divide the filling equally between the pastry circles. With a pastry brush, dampen the edges of the circles with a little water. Fold the pastry to form a semi-circle and press the edges together to seal.
8. Place the pies on a non-stick baking sheet, lightly brush with water and dust with the paprika. Bake in the oven for about 15–18 minutes.

Points per serving: 6
Total Points per recipe: 36

Fabulous Puddings

When you're watching your waistline, your sweet tooth doesn't simply disappear – you still need to be able to treat yourself once in a while! This chapter is full of delicious puddings that are perfect just for that. Recipes such as Eton Mess, Cinnamon Pavlova with Pears and Blackcurrants and Quick Peach Ice Cream are all a dream for dessert lovers and they'll spoil you, not your diet!

Eton Mess

Serves 4

Preparation time: 5 minutes
Calories per serving: 155

Freezing: not recommended

Named after the famous school and based on the dessert traditionally served at prize-giving day, this is as light and tasty as a dream.

360 g (12 oz) low-fat fromage frais or low-fat natural yogurt
213 g can of blackcurrants in natural juice, drained
290 g can of raspberries in natural juice, drained
4 small meringue nests, broken into bite-sized pieces

1. Gently fold all the ingredients together, reserving some fruit to decorate.
2. Spoon into serving glasses and top with extra fruit to decorate, adding any extra Points as necessary.

Points per serving: with fromage frais 3; with low-fat natural yogurt 2½
Total Points per recipe: with fromage frais 12; with low-fat natural yogurt 10

Rapid Rice Pudding

Serves 4

Preparation time: 5 minutes
Cooking time: 40 minutes
Calories per serving: 360

Freezing: not recommended

This is a Spanish-style rice pudding. Serve with or without fresh fruit.

180 g (6 oz) pudding rice
1 litre (1¾ pints) skimmed milk
120 g (4 oz) dried apricots, chopped
60 g (2 oz) sultanas
1 bay leaf
½ teaspoon ground nutmeg
grated zest and juice of 1 orange
15 g (½ oz) soft brown sugar
ground cinnamon

1. Place the rice, milk, apricots, sultanas, bay leaf, nutmeg, orange zest and juice and sugar in a medium non-stick saucepan. Heat this rice mixture until it is almost boiling. Then reduce the heat and gently simmer, uncovered, for 30–40 minutes or until the rice is tender. Ensure you stir the rice occasionally to prevent it from sticking and, if the pan becomes too dry, add a little more milk.
2. This rice pudding can be served warm or chilled, spooned into bowls and sprinkled with a little cinnamon.

Points per serving: 5
Total Points per recipe: 20

Warm Plum Cake

Serves 6

Preparation time: 10 minutes
Cooking time: 20 minutes
Calories per serving: 170

Freezing: not recommended

The plums give this such a luscious texture. Try to eat this cake when it is warm and at its best.

low-fat cooking spray
1 orange, washed and quartered
567 g can of plums, stoned and drained
210 g packet of low-fat sponge mix

1. Preheat the oven to Gas Mark 6/200°C/400°F. Lightly spray a 1.2-litre (2-pint) shallow, ovenproof dish. Boil the orange until soft and then process it to a smooth purée.
2. Spoon the plums and 6 tablespoons of their juice into the bottom of the dish.
3. Make the sponge mixture according to the packet instructions. Fold the puréed orange into this sponge mixture and spoon it over the plums.
4. Bake in the oven for 15–20 minutes, or until golden brown and firm. Serve straight from the dish, or turn the pudding out and dust lightly with icing sugar.

Points per serving: 3
Total Points per recipe: 18

Pear and Muscovado Tarts

Serves 4

Preparation time: 5 minutes
Cooking time: 12 minutes
Calories per serving: 250; with fromage frais 255

Freezing: not recommended

Serve these easy fruit tarts with low-fat fromage frais or low-fat natural yogurt. Remember to add the extra Points.

22 g (3/4 oz) polyunsaturated margarine, melted
4 medium slices of bread
60 g (2 oz) muscovado sugar
822 g can pear halves in natural juice, drained and sliced thickly
1 large banana, sliced thinly

1. Preheat the oven to Gas Mark 7/200°C/400°F.
2. Brush a little melted margarine over each slice of bread. Sprinkle a small amount of the sugar over the top and place each slice on a non-stick baking tray.
3. Arrange the pear slices on each slice of bread, working from the outside to the centre. Then place the banana slices in the centre. (Note – make sure you cover all the bread, otherwise it will burn.)
4. Sprinkle the remaining sugar over each slice of bread, ensuring the fruit is well covered, and bake in the oven for 10–12 minutes or until golden and bubbling hot.
5. Serve the tarts straight from the oven, on their own, or with a spoonful of low-fat fromage frais or low-fat natural yogurt.

Points per serving: 4
Total Points per recipe: 16

Banana and Pear Bread Pudding

Serves 4

Preparation time: 10 minutes
Cooking time: 45 minutes
Calories per serving: 375

Freezing: not recommended

A delicious low-fat version of the classic 'bread-and-butter pudding', with an unusual topping of bananas and pears. It can be put together in minutes and looks gorgeous when it puffs up and browns.

2 large ripe bananas, sliced
415 g can of pears in natural juice, drained and sliced
8 medium slices of Granary bread, cut into fingers, or French stick with crust about 2.5 cm (1-inch) thick
600 ml (1 pint) skimmed milk
2 large eggs
2 tablespoons runny honey or pure maple syrup
1/2 teaspoon ground nutmeg
1 1/2 teaspoons ground cinnamon
a little icing sugar, to dust

1. Preheat the oven to Gas Mark 5/190°C/375°F.
2. Place half the bananas and pears in a 1.75-litre (3-pint) ovenproof dish. Arrange the bread slices on top and scatter with the remaining fruit.
3. Whisk together the milk, eggs, honey and nutmeg. Pour over the bread and fruit, pushing down to soak up the liquid. Dust the top with the cinnamon and a little icing sugar.
4. Bake in the oven for 40–45 minutes or until the pudding is slightly browned and puffy and the liquid has been absorbed. For extra browning, the pudding can be placed under a grill for a few minutes. Serve hot or warm.

Points per serving: 6 1/2 with Granary; 5 with French bread
Total Points per recipe: 26 with Granary; 20 with French bread

Cinnamon Pavlova with Pears and Blackcurrants

Serves 4

Preparation time: 10 minutes
Cooking time: 50 minutes
Calories per serving: 275

Freezing: not recommended

A delicious cinnamon meringue, topped with fromage frais and fruit.

3 egg whites
180 g (6 oz) caster sugar
2 teaspoons ground cinnamon
1 teaspoon cornflour
1/2 teaspoon vinegar
360 g (12 oz) virtually-fat-free fromage frais
415 g can of pears in natural juice, drained and sliced
213 g can of blackcurrants in natural juice, drained

1. Preheat the oven to Gas Mark 2/150°C/300°F. Line a baking tray with baking parchment.
2. In a large bowl, whisk the egg whites until stiff. Gradually whisk in the sugar, a tablespoon at a time, whisking well between each addition. Using a large metal spoon, gently fold in the ground cinnamon, cornflour and vinegar.
3. Pile the mixture into 4 heaps on the prepared baking tray and shape into 4 rounds, hollowing a dip in the middle of each. Bake in the oven for 40–50 minutes or until golden and firm on the outside and soft in the centre. Allow to cool on the baking tray for 5 minutes before serving.
4. To serve, place each pavlova on an individual plate and top with some fromage frais and a serving of pears and blackcurrants. Serve at once.

Points per serving: 4 1/2
Total Points per recipe: 18

Apricot and Raspberry Soup

Serves 4

Preparation time: 10 minutes
Calories per serving: 150

Freezing: not recommended

This tasty dessert is ready in minutes!

2 × 411 g can of apricots in natural juice
150 ml (1/4 pint) orange juice
240 g (8 oz) frozen raspberries, slightly thawed
4 tablespoons low-fat fromage frais or low-fat natural yogurt
60 g (2 oz) toasted flaked almonds

1. Liquidise the apricots in their juice and the orange juice, until smooth.
2. To serve, pour the apricot purée into individual serving bowls and place a heaped tablespoon of raspberries in the centre of each bowl. Thin the fromage frais or yogurt with a little water and swirl a spoonful on to each bowl. Finally, scatter on the toasted almonds and serve.

Points per serving: with yogurt 2½; with fromage frais 3½
Total Points per recipe: with yogurt 10; with fromage frais 14

Quick Peach Ice Cream

Serves 4

Preparation time: 5 minutes
Calories per serving: 95

Freezing: not recommended

This is a simple way of making fruity ice cream and is best when freshly made.

415 g can of sliced peaches in natural juice
2 teaspoons runny honey
360 g (12 oz) low-fat plain fromage frais

1. In a shallow, freezerproof container, freeze the peaches with their juice until almost solid.
2. Tip the frozen peaches into a food processor and whizz very briefly. Add the honey and fromage frais and whizz again, until just smooth but still ice cold.
3. Serve at once or freeze until required but make sure you remove it from the freezer at least 20–30 minutes before serving.

Points per serving: 2½
Total Points per recipe: 10

Rhubarb, Strawberry and Orange Cobbler

Serves 6

Preparation time: 10 minutes
Cooking time: 25 minutes
Calories per serving: 225

Freezing: not recommended

Cobblers are perfect for dessert any time and this one is full of flavour. You'll love it.

410 g can of strawberries in natural juice
539 g can of rhubarb in syrup, drained
2 large oranges, peeled and segmented
213 g can of blackcurrants in natural juice, drained
1 fresh rosemary sprig (optional)

For the topping:

150 g (5 oz) self-raising flour
1 teaspoon baking powder
a pinch of salt
22 g (3/4 oz) brown sugar
grated zest and juice of 1 small lemon or orange
about 6 tablespoons semi-skimmed milk
22 g (3/4 oz) polyunsaturated margarine, melted

1. Preheat the oven to Gas Mark 6/200°C/400°F.
2. In a food processor or liquidiser, purée the strawberries, with their juice, until smooth.
3. In a large bowl, gently mix together the rhubarb, oranges, blackcurrants, strawberry purée and rosemary (if using). Turn the fruit mixture into a 1.75-litre (3-pint) shallow, ovenproof dish. Set to one side.
4. For the scone topping, sift the flour, baking powder and salt together in a bowl. Stir in the sugar and orange or lemon zest. Mix together half the milk with the melted margarine and orange juice, and add to the flour mixture.
5. Briefly combine the ingredients, adding extra milk to obtain a dropping consistency. Drop 6 spoonfuls of the mixture over the fruit.
6. Bake the cobbler in the oven for 25–30 minutes or until bubbling hot and golden brown. Lightly dust with icing sugar and serve.

Points per serving: 3
Total Points per recipe: 18

Oriental Baked Fruit Salad

Serves 4

Preparation time: 10 minutes
Cooking time: 30 minutes
Calories per serving: 190

Freezing: not recommended

Here's an exciting change from the usual fruit salad. Chinese five-spice powder, available from larger supermarkets and oriental shops, is the secret of the fabulous flavour in this dessert. Canned melon balls can be used in place of the mango.

1 eating apple, peeled, cored and sliced thinly
2 medium bananas, sliced thickly
400 g can of mango slices in syrup, drained
425 g can of lychees, drained, with syrup reserved
grated zest and juice of 1 lemon
1/2 teaspoon Chinese five-spice powder
1 bay leaf
1 teaspoon finely chopped fresh root ginger
1 tablespoon finely chopped fresh mint (optional)

1. Preheat the oven to Gas Mark 5/190°C/375°F.
2. Place all the prepared fruits in a large casserole dish.
3. Combine the lemon zest and juice with the Chinese spices, bay leaf, ginger and lychee syrup and pour over the fruit.
4. Bake for 20–30 minutes until bubbling and hot. Stir in the mint and serve at once.

Points per serving: 2 1/2
Total Points per recipe: 10

Cherry Berry Grunts

Serves 6

Preparation time: 10 minutes
Cooking time: 30 minutes
Calories per serving: 305

Freezing: not recommended

The grated carrot gives this deliciously rich pudding extra moistness and sweetness.

low-fat cooking spray
425 g can of cherries in natural juice, drained
287 g can of blackberries in natural juice, drained (juice reserved)
60 g (2 oz) polyunsaturated margarine
60 g (2 oz) soft brown sugar
180 g (6 oz) fresh brown breadcrumbs
1 teaspoon baking powder
1 teaspoon ground nutmeg
1 egg, separated
1 carrot, grated
6 tablespoons skimmed milk
icing sugar, to decorate
6 tablespoons low-fat fromage frais

1. Preheat the oven to Gas Mark 5/190°C/375°F. Lightly spray 6 ramekins, or ovenproof teacups, with spray oil.
2. Mix together the cherries and blackberries. Place some of this mixture and 2 tablespoons of the reserved blackberry juice into each ramekin.
3. In a mixing bowl, beat the polyunsaturated margarine and sugar together until soft. Add the breadcrumbs, baking powder and nutmeg. Now stir in the egg yolk, carrot and milk.
4. Whisk the egg white until stiff and fold into the mixture. Spoon the mixture equally into the 6 ramekins ensuring the fruit is covered. Bake the grunts in the oven for 25–30 minutes or until risen and firm.
5. Dust with icing sugar and serve the berry grunts immediately, with 1 tablespoon of fromage frais per serving. Alternatively, allow to cool in the ramekins for 5 minutes before carefully turning out.

Points per serving: 5
Total Points per recipe: 30

Plum and Blackcurrant Pancake Pie

Serves 6

Preparation and cooking time: 15 minutes
Calories per serving: 215
Freezing: not recommended

A lovely combination of fruits, fromage frais and chocolate pancakes. Assemble this dessert just before serving.

For the batter:
60 g (2 oz) plain flour
1 tablespoon cocoa powder
1 egg
150 ml (1/4 pint) skimmed milk
1/2 tablespoon sunflower oil
a little oil, for greasing
For the filling:
567 g can of plums in natural juice, stoned, drained and halved
213 g can of blackcurrants in natural juice, drained
2 large bananas, sliced thickly
1 teaspoon ground cinnamon
vanilla essence, to taste
360 g (12 oz) low-fat fromage frais

1. In a large bowl, beat together the flour, cocoa powder, egg, milk, and oil until smooth.
2. Heat a non-stick frying-pan. Add a little oil and wipe out with kitchen paper. Pour enough batter into the pan to just coat the base. Cook for 1 minute, then loosen the edges, turn over, and cook the other side. Continue until you have 4 pancakes. Leave to cool.
3. Next, make the filling. In a bowl, gently combine the plums, blackcurrants and bananas with the cinnamon. In another bowl, add a few drops of vanilla essence to the fromage frais.
4. To assemble the pancake pie, put the first pancake on a plate. Spread with a thin layer of the fromage frais mixture and top with some fruit. Continue to layer, finishing with a layer of fromage frais and fruit. Cut into wedges and serve immediately, or chill until required.

Points per serving: 4
Total Points per recipe: 24

Delicious Bakes

Home-baking certainly shouldn't be a thing of the past. You are far better off baking your own goodies, since bakery goods from the shop tend to be very high in saturated fats and sugars. This chapter has easy-to-make recipes which won't let you slave over a hot stove.

Brownies

Makes 8

Preparation time: 10 minutes
Cooking time: 40 minutes
Calories per brownie: 170; with Low-fat frosting 1, 185; with Low-fat frosting 2, 180

Freezing: not recommended

An old favourite – ideal for chocolate-lovers.

150 g (5 oz) low-fat soft cheese
180 g (6 oz) muscovado or soft brown sugar
45 g (1½ oz) cocoa powder
2 egg whites
1 teaspoon vanilla essence
1 tablespoon semi-skimmed milk
60 g (2 oz) plain flour
½ teaspoon baking powder

1. Preheat the oven to Gas Mark 4/180°C/350°F. Line a 15 cm (6-inch) square tin with baking parchment.
2. In a large bowl, combine the cheese with the sugar. Add the cocoa powder, egg whites, vanilla essence and milk. Beat well until smooth.
3. Sift the flour and baking powder into the cheese mixture and fold in lightly.
4. Pour the mixture into the prepared tin and bake in the oven for 30–40 minutes until just set.
5. Remove from the oven and allow to cool in the tin. Serve cut into squares, topped with one of the low-fat frostings below, if desired.

Low-fat frosting 1
60 g (2 oz) low-fat soft cheese
1 tablespoon low-fat natural yogurt or fromage frais
½ tablespoon drinking chocolate powder
In a bowl, combine all the ingredients together and spread on top of the brownies.

Low-fat frosting 2
3 tablespoons low-fat natural yogurt
1 tablespoon drinking chocolate powder
Top the brownies with the yogurt and sprinkle with drinking chocolate powder.

Points per brownie: 2½, with either Low-fat frosting 3
Total Points per recipe: 20, with either Low-fat frosting 24

Cinnamon Cookies

Makes 10

Preparation and cooking time: 20 minutes
Calories per cookie: 160

Freezing: not recommended

These speedy biscuits are excellent served with warm fruit salad or ice cream.

120 g (4 oz) polyunsaturated margarine
60 g (2 oz) brown sugar
grated zest of 1 lemon
150 g (5 oz) self-raising flour
3 teaspoons ground cinnamon
icing sugar, to decorate

1. Preheat the oven to Gas Mark 5/190°C/375°F.
2. In a mixing bowl, cream together the margarine, sugar and lemon zest. Stir in the flour and cinnamon. Mix well.
3. Divide the mixture into 10 and roll with your hands into rounds. Then place on a lightly floured baking tray.
4. Flatten the cookies with a wet fork and bake for 10–15 minutes.
5. Allow to cool slightly before placing on a wire rack. Dust with icing sugar before serving warm or cold.

Points per cookie: 3
Total Points per recipe: 30

Apple and Raisin Muffins

Makes 12

Preparation time: 10 minutes
Cooking time: 20–25 minutes
Calories per muffin: 155

Freezing: not recommended

Home-cooking at its best!

low-fat cooking spray
120 g (4 oz) porridge oats
210 ml (7 fl oz) semi-skimmed milk
180 g (6 oz) plain flour
[illegible] teaspoons baking powder
1 teaspoon ground cinnamon
½ teaspoon ground nutmeg
30 g (1 oz) soft brown sugar
4 tablespoons low-fat natural yogurt
2 large eggs, beaten
1 large eating apple, peeled, cored and diced
90 g (3 oz) sultanas or raisins
a pinch of salt

1. Preheat the oven to Gas Mark 6/200°C/400°F. Spray a 12-hole muffin tin.
2. In a large bowl, mix together the oats and milk. Set to one side.
3. In another bowl, sift together the flour, baking powder, cinnamon, nutmeg and a pinch of salt. Stir in the sugar.
4. Add the yogurt and eggs to the oats and mix well. Then add the dry ingredients to the oat mixture along with the diced apple and sultanas. Fold together until just combined.
5. Spoon the mixture into the greased tin and bake for 20–25 minutes.
6. Allow the muffins to cool in the tin for 5 minutes before transferring to a wire rack.

Points per serving: 2½
Total Points per recipe: 30

Quick Orange and Lemon Cake

Serves 6

Preparation time: 10 minutes
Cooking time: 45 minutes
Calories per serving: 280

Freezing: not recommended

A very moist and delicious dessert-style cake.

low-fat cooking spray
420 g can of chick-peas, drained and rinsed
3 eggs
210 g (7 oz) sugar
[illegible] teaspoon baking powder
grated zest and juice of 1 orange
grated zest and juice of 1 lemon
90 g (3 oz) sultanas or raisins
icing sugar and cinnamon, to decorate

1. Preheat the oven to Gas Mark 4/180°C/350°F. Spray a 20 cm (8-inch) cake tin with low-fat cooking spray and line the base with greaseproof paper.
2. In a food processor, blend the chick-peas until smooth. Add the eggs, sugar, baking powder and orange and lemon zest. Mix briefly until all the ingredients are combined. Stir in the sultanas or raisins.
3. Turn the mixture into the prepared cake tin and bake for 35–45 minutes or until golden. The cake is cooked when a knife is inserted into the centre and comes out clean.
4. Spoon the orange and lemon juices over the cake and allow the cake to cool in the tin for 10 minutes, before transferring to a wire rack. When the cake is cool, dredge with the icing sugar and cinnamon.

Points per serving: 4½
Total Points per recipe: 27

Index

apple and raisin muffins **79**
apple cobbler, pork and **63**
apple frittata, potato, ham and **10**
apples and bacon, pasta bows with **56**
apricot and raspberry soup **71**

banana and pear bread pudding **68**
bean and chicken pies, mustard **63**
bean stew, Mexican-style **27**
borlotti salad **36**
broccoli soup, mint, pea and **28**
brownies **76**
bubble and squeak with mushroom râgout **55**
bulgar wheat and salsa, meat patties with **56**
burgers, chick-pea **12**
butter bean chilli tacos **8**
butter bean soup, garlic and **23**

cake, quick orange and lemon **79**
cake, warm plum **67**
cherry berry grunts **75**
chicken pies, mustard, bean and **63**
chicken tikka salad, warm **31**
chicken with orange and dill **52**
chick-pea burgers **12**
chips, low-fat **40**
cinnamon cookies **76**
cinnamon pavlova with pears and blackcurrants **68**
clams, linguine with peppers and **51**
crab cakes with spicy cucumber relish **39**

de luxe pasta râgout **24**
dill sauce, salmon muffins with **48**
dumplings, parsnip and pepper goulash with **27**

eggs with ratatouille **16**
eton mess **64**

fast salmon pâté **15**
filo pastry, smoked haddock in **43**
fish and string bean korma **43**
frittata, potato, ham and apple **10**
fruit salad, Oriental baked **72**

gado gado, vegetable **32**
garlic and butter bean soup **23**
garlic toasts **19**
goulash, parsnip and pepper, with dumplings **27**
grilled salmon fillets **40**

haddock, roasted, with herbs **47**
haddock, smoked, in filo pastry **43**
haggis, lentil and mushroom **60**
ham and apple frittata, potato, **10**

ice cream, quick peach **71**

jacket potato salad **31**

lamb and herb meatloaf **60**
lattice potatoes **10**
lemon cake, quick orange and **79**
lentil and mushroom haggis **60**
lentil *sag* **59**
linguine with peppers and clams **51**
low-fat chips **40**

meatloaf, lamb and herb **60**
meat patties with bulgar wheat and salsa **56**
mediterranean pizza salad **35**
Mexican sauce, tortilla with **15**
Mexican-style bean stew **27**
mint, pea and broccoli soup **28**
muffin toasts, sardine **12**
muffins, apple and raisin **79**
muffins, salmon, with dill sauce **48**
mushroom râgout, bubble and squeak with **55**
mustard, bean and chicken pies **63**

ocean pizza pie **44**
omelette with spinach, tomatoes and cheese **19**
orange and dill, chicken with **52**
orange and lemon cake, quick **79**
Oriental baked fruit salad **72**
Oriental salad **36**

paella, pasta **44**
pancake pie, plum and blackcurrant **75**
parsnip and pepper goulash with dumplings **27**
pasta bows with apples and bacon **56**
pasta paella **44**
pasta râgout, de luxe **24**
pâté, white bean, with horseradish **16**
pea and broccoli soup, mint, **28**
peach ice cream, quick **71**
pear and muscovado tarts **67**
pear bread pudding, banana and **68**
pear, poppy seed and cheese bap **8**
pears and blackcurrants, cinnamon pavlova with **68**
peppers and clams, linguine with **51**
pizza pie, ocean **44**
pizza salad, Mediterranean **35**
plum and blackcurrant pancake pie **75**
plum cake, warm **67**
pork and apple cobbler **63**
potato, bacon and apple hot-pot **23**
potato, ham and apple frittata **10**
potato salad, jacket **31**
potatoes, lattice **10**

quick orange and lemon cake **79**
quick peach ice cream **71**
quick salmon kedgeree **47**

raisin and mint raita **59**
rapid rice pudding **64**
raspberry soup, apricot and **71**
rhubarb, strawberry and orange cobbler **72**
rice pudding, rapid **64**
roasted haddock with herbs **47**

salad, borlotti **36**
salad, jacket potato **31**
salad, Mediterranean pizza **35**
salad, Oriental **36**
salad, warm chicken tikka **31**
salade Niçoise with salmon **35**
salmon fillets, grilled **40**
salmon kedgeree, quick **47**
salmon muffins with dill sauce **48**
salmon pâté, fast **15**
sardine muffin toasts **12**
scotch broth **24**
seafood soup **20**
smoked haddock in filo pastry **43**
soup, apricot and raspberry **71**
soup, garlic and butter bean **23**
soup, mint, pea and broccoli **28**
soup, seafood **20**
soup, Thai-style **28**
spicy cucumber relish, crab cakes with **39**
spinach, tomatoes and cheese, omelette with **19**
stir-fry teriyaki vegetables **55**
strawberry and orange cobbler, rhubarb **72**
string bean korma, fish and **43**

tacos, butter bean chilli **8**
teriyaki tuna steaks with ginger and garlic **51**
teriyaki vegetables, stir-fry **55**
Thai-style soup **28**
toasts, garlic **19**
tomato, red pepper and spinach pies **52**
tortilla with Mexican sauce **15**
tuna steaks with ginger and garlic, teriyaki **51**

vegetable gado gado **32**
vegetables, stir-fry teriyaki **55**

warm chicken tikka salad **31**
warm plum cake **67**
white bean pâté with horseradish **16**